Serious Student/Parent Comprehensive Guide to the AI-Based College Application Process

"How to Successfully Navigate the Recruitment Process in the New World of AI"

Tiffanee Charles-Hockaday MS

Claude Louis-Charles PhD

Cybersoft Publishing LLC

Fort Washington, MD 20744

First Edition March 2026

Table of Contents

Introduction

College recruitment is not what it used to be. For today's juniors and seniors, the process doesn't start with a glossy brochure landing in the mailbox or a single college fair in the gym. It starts quietly—often without anyone realizing it—the moment a student clicks "learn more" on a website, fills out a short interest form, or watches a campus tour on their phone. Behind those simple actions lie powerful AI systems that track patterns, make predictions, and help colleges decide who to notice, when to reach out, and how to spend scarce scholarship dollars.

For many families, that reality feels unsettling. Parents who went to college themselves remember a process that, while stressful, was at least understandable. You knew when your application was due, who your guidance counselor was, and where the thick or thin envelope would show up. Today, the rules are less obvious. Emails appear to be surprisingly personal, even when no human ever typed them. Chatbots answer late-night questions better than some brochures. Portals suggest majors and "best fit" programs, as if they already know your student's story. It's hard not to wonder: Who is really in the driver's seat here—us, or the algorithms?

This book exists to help you answer that question with clarity and confidence. It doesn't try to scare you about AI, and it doesn't pretend AI is just another fad you can ignore. Instead, it treats AI as what it has already become in college admissions: a permanent part of the landscape, one that can either quietly disadvantage your student or quietly amplify their strengths, depending on how aware and intentional your family is. The goal is not to turn teenagers into data scientists or parents into programmers. The goal is to give you enough understanding to protect your options, avoid avoidable mistakes, and use technology as a helping hand instead of a hidden judge.

This perspective comes from experience on the inside. For more than a decade, I've sat on the other side of the emails, tours, and application files as a college recruiter and admissions professional. I've spent years visiting high schools, meeting with counselors, reading applications by the thousands, and talking with families at kitchen tables and in crowded auditoriums. I've worked with students from large suburban schools with multiple counselors, and with students from small or under-resourced schools where the "college office" is a single person wearing five different hats. I've seen what families assume is happening behind the scenes—and how different the reality often is.

My background isn't just practical; it's also grounded in education. I hold a Master's degree in Higher Education, which means I've studied how students learn, how systems are designed, and how policies affect real people. That training changed the way I look at admissions. I don't see recruitment as a series of one-off interactions; I see it as a system that either opens doors or quietly closes them. When AI and predictive analytics began entering that system—first through basic data tools, then through more advanced platforms—I watched how quickly the "rules of the game" shifted, often without students or parents realizing anything had changed.

In the early years of my recruiting career, "data" mostly meant spreadsheets and basic reports. We tracked where applications came from, which events were popular, and which high schools produced the most enrollments. Those reports helped us plan travel routes and decide which programs to promote. But gradually, the tools became smarter. Instead of just telling us what had happened, they started telling us what might happen next: which students were "likely to apply," which were "likely to enroll," and which should receive a personal phone call because they were "on the fence." At first, these predictions felt like handy suggestions. Over time, they began to shape how offices spent their limited time and attention quietly.

That shift has very real consequences for families. When a system flags one student as “high priority” and another as “low engagement,” it often means one gets more touchpoints, more invitations, and sometimes more access to special programs or scholarships. Those differences are not always based on merit or potential; sometimes they are based on who has reliable internet, who filled out a certain survey, or whose school was already on the college’s radar. As a recruiter, I saw how easily students could fall through the cracks—not because they weren’t strong candidates, but because their “digital shadow” didn’t look like what the algorithms were trained to expect.

That’s why this book takes a very specific stance: AI should be treated as a **trusted** assistant, not the star of the show. Students should never use AI to write their story, impersonate their voice, or shortcut the hard work of reflecting on who they are and what they want. Parents should never assume that because a system is “smart,” it is always fair or always right. At the same time, ignoring AI entirely is no longer realistic. The colleges your student is considering are already using it—to find students, to organize information, and sometimes to forecast who is “worth” extra attention. Families who understand that can make better choices, ask sharper questions, and keep the human parts of this process front and center.

Throughout these chapters, we’ll walk step by step through the different ways AI shows up in the admissions journey: in how colleges recruit, how they build digital profiles of students, how they personalize outreach, and how they assess everything from essays to "demonstrated interest." At each stage, you'll see three things: what's actually happening behind the scenes, how those systems can help or hurt, and how to use AI on your own side in an ethical, student-centered way. You'll hear stories from the road—moments in school auditoriums, late-night emails from anxious parents, quiet conversations with students who didn't think anyone would notice them—and we'll connect those stories to the technology shaping this new era.

Most importantly, every chapter ends with a "Checklist for Action" tailored separately for students and for parents. This isn't theory for theory's sake. It's a practical guide built to sit on your kitchen table, next to the laptop and the stack of flyers, so that you can turn information into concrete steps. By the time you reach the end, I hope that you'll feel less like the admissions process is happening to you and more like you—and your student—are active participants, capable of working alongside AI instead of being quietly judged by it.

1 The New Era of College Recruitment

1.1 Monday Morning in the Admissions Office

By 8:15 a.m., the admissions office is already humming. Laptops flip open, coffee cups hit the desks, and a wall of screens begins lighting up with dashboards. Instead of paper files stacked in milk crates or color-coded folders spread across a conference table, a recruiting coordinator logs into a system that shows live “heat maps” of student interest across the country. Overnight, hundreds of high school juniors clicked on virtual campus tours, opened financial aid emails, and saved majors to their wish lists.

At the center of the room, a counselor pauses at one particular dashboard. A student from Maryland has opened every email from the university in the last week, spent fifteen minutes on the engineering page, and filled out a "request information" form at 11:47 p.m. The system quietly flags: "High engagement. First-generation likelihood: high. Predicted enrollment probability if admitted: 72%." No one in that office has ever met this student, but the college's AI-powered system already has a working picture of who they might be, what they care about, and how likely they are to say "yes" if offered a place.

This is the new normal. Instead of starting their day with a stack of paper applications, admissions teams now start with data streams and predictions. The work of recruiting hasn't disappeared; it has shifted. People still read essays, answer calls, and visit high schools—but they do it guided by algorithms that prioritize which students to reach first. For families, that means the quiet decisions made by invisible systems can shape who gets noticed, when outreach happens, and what opportunities are offered long before an application is even submitted.

THEN: TRADITIONAL ADMISSIONS

THEN: TRADITIONAL ADMISSIONS

NOW: AI-DRIVEN RECRUITMENT

NOW: AI-DRIVEN RECRUITMENT

1.2 From Gut Feel to Data Signals

For decades, college recruitment leaned heavily on geography and gut instinct. Admissions officers would say things like, “We always recruit heavily in this region,” or “This high school sends us strong students.” Decisions about where to travel, which students to invite to special programs, and how many brochures to print were based on past patterns and personal judgment. That approach wasn’t always fair, but it felt familiar. Families could see the process: the college fair, the postcard, the counselor visit.

Now, recruitment is increasingly driven by data signals and predictive models. When a student clicks on a link in an email, stays on a specific page, or signs up for a webinar, those actions are quietly recorded in customer-relationship systems designed specifically for higher education. These systems don’t just store information; they continually analyze it. They look for patterns: Which students who attended last year’s virtual tour actually applied? Which students who downloaded the engineering brochure ended up enrolling? Over time, the software learns to recognize behaviors that suggest serious interest versus casual curiosity.

This shift doesn’t mean human judgment has disappeared. It means human judgment is being guided, and sometimes constrained, by the patterns of the algorithms' surface. Recruiters might still choose to visit a school because of a long-standing relationship. Still, they now see a report showing how many students from that school opened emails last year and whether they ultimately enrolled. For some students, this new reality opens doors: a student in a small or rural school might come to the radar simply because their engagement data stands out. For others, especially those less comfortable engaging online, the absence of digital signals can mean fewer touches and invitations.

1.3 How AI Quietly Enters the Admissions Pipeline

Most families never see the moment AI enters the admissions pipeline because it happens behind logins and within software systems with brand-safe names. A college may call its platform "Student Success Hub" or "Enrollment Insights," but beneath the friendly labels are machine-learning models that score and sort thousands of potential applicants. These tools do not decide who is admitted—that still falls to people—but they strongly influence who gets attention, who receives follow-up, and which students are labeled "high priority."

Modern recruiting systems typically combine several layers of AI. One model might estimate a student's likelihood of applying based on academic interests, location, and engagement with the college website. Another model might predict the chance that the student will enroll if admitted—a key number known as "yield probability." Yet another algorithm might recommend the best next action: send a personalized email, invite to a major-specific webinar, or have a counselor make a phone call. Each of these predictions nudges admissions staff toward investing more time in some students than others.

From a student's perspective, all of this can feel like sudden, intense attention. A string of messages arrives: "We'd love to see you at our STEM Open House," "Based on your interests, you might enjoy hearing from current engineering students," "Here's a scholarship you may qualify for." It feels personal because, in a sense, it is. The system is using what it has learned about that student's behavior and academic profile to tailor outreach. But it's important to understand that this personal touch is powered by pattern-recognition and probability, not by someone in an office sitting and writing to one individual at a time.

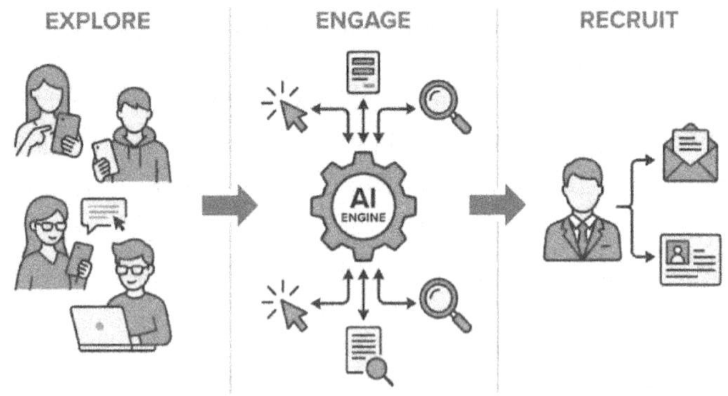

1.4 What This Means for Students

For students, this new era of AI-driven recruitment changes the "starting line." In the past, the process seemed to begin when you decided to apply. Today, it effectively begins the moment you start interacting with colleges online—sometimes as early as ninth or tenth grade. Your clicks, sign-ups, and survey responses can all become signals that shape how colleges view you long before you might think of yourself as an applicant. That doesn't mean every move is being scored like a game, but it does mean your digital choices can either make you more visible or leave you in the background.

One practical impact is that "demonstrated interest" now has both a human and an algorithmic side. When you attend an information session, send a thoughtful question, or visit campus, you show interest in a way admissions officers can see and remember. At the same time, the systems tracking your behavior are adding up smaller, quieter actions: Did you watch that virtual tour video to the end? Did you open the financial aid email? Did you return to the same major page more than once? Taken together, these actions tell a story about your seriousness—and that story can influence who receives more communication and, in some cases, how admission officers read an application.

This can feel intimidating, especially when you're already juggling school, activities, and life. The reassuring truth is that you don't have to become a full-time marketer of yourself. You do, however, benefit from understanding that your digital behavior sends signals, whether you mean it to or not. Instead of passively letting those signals accumulate, you can make small, intentional choices that align with your genuine interests: signing up for information from colleges that truly fit you, opening and reading messages you care about, and participating in events that help you decide whether a campus belongs on your list.

1.5 What This Means for Parents

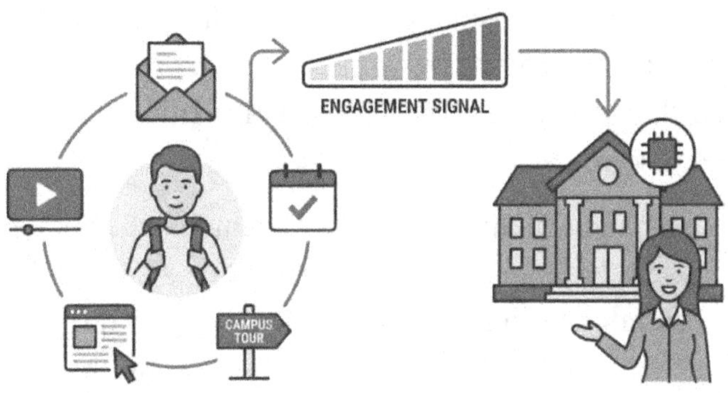

For parents, the shift to AI-driven recruitment can create a mix of relief and anxiety. On one hand, you might appreciate that colleges have more tools to identify strong matches for your student, especially if you live in an area that doesn't get many in-person visits. On the other hand, it can be unsettling to realize that unseen systems are constantly "reading" your student's behavior and making predictions about their future choices. You may wonder: What exactly are they tracking? Are these tools fair? And how do I guide my teenager without turning every click into a high-stakes decision?

A helpful starting point is to remember that colleges aren't using AI to spy on students; they're using it because they are under pressure. Recruitment offices have to meet enrollment targets, balance their classes by major and geography, and manage budgets—all while dealing with application surges and shifting demographics. AI helps them manage volume and uncertainty. But like any tool, its impact depends on how carefully it is used and how aware families are of its influence. Your role is not to micromanage every online move but to help your student understand the big picture and make choices with eyes open.

That may mean having new kinds of conversations at the dinner table. Instead of just asking, "Did you finish your essay?" you might ask, "Which colleges have you actually engaged with this week?" Instead of doing everything for your student behind the scenes, you can coach them to take ownership of their digital presence: reading emails, signing up for relevant events, and asking questions when something feels confusing or pushy. The goal is not to outsmart the algorithms but to ensure your student's authentic interests show up clearly in a system that increasingly relies on digital traces.

1.6 The "Marketplace" Your Student Is Entering

One of the most important things to understand is that college recruitment has become more like a marketplace. In that marketplace, students are not just choosing colleges; colleges are choosing where to invest their time, attention, and financial aid dollars. AI helps them decide which students are most likely to enroll, succeed academically, and persist to graduation. That means your student is, in a sense, being "scored" as a potential match, not only based on grades and test scores but also on patterns of behavior and fit.

In this environment, visibility matters. Students who show consistent, genuine engagement with a college tend to rise higher on outreach lists than those who appear only once, for example, through a test score report. Students who respond to messages, attend events, and complete forms on time are easier for algorithms to understand than students whose data is thin or inconsistent. This doesn't replace the importance of academic preparation or personal character, but it adds another layer to how colleges decide where to focus their limited attention.

Families who understand this marketplace can make more informed choices. Instead of applying to a dozen schools with minimal interaction, you might encourage your student to engage more deeply with a smaller set of schools that truly fit their needs. Instead of ignoring every email that looks automated, your student can learn to scan subject lines for important opportunities—like special programs or early scholarship information. By recognizing that AI is helping colleges manage a crowded marketplace, you can help your student show up in that space in a way that reflects who they really are.

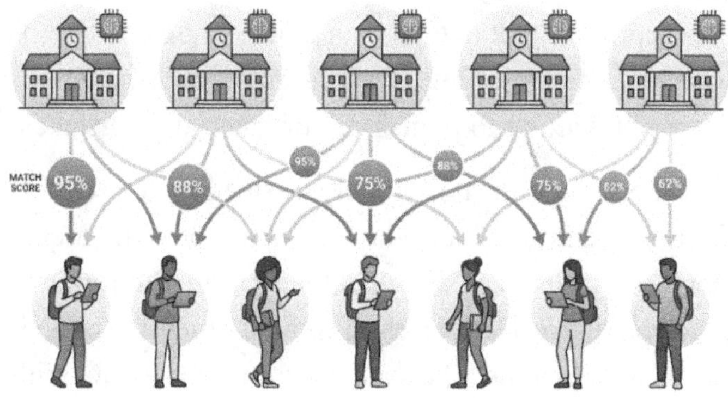

1.7 Common Misconceptions About AI in Recruitment

As AI becomes more visible in headlines, families often hold assumptions that don't align with reality about how most colleges use these tools. Some students fear that "the computer decides everything" and that humans no longer read applications. Others assume that if they don't use AI themselves, they'll be left behind by peers using every new tool they can find. Clearing up these misunderstandings early helps everyone approach the process with less panic and more strategy.

One widespread misconception is that AI can "see" everything about a student—every text message, every social media post, every late-night search. In reality, college systems are typically limited to the data students and schools provide, such as contact forms, test score submissions, interactions with official websites, and information from authorized partners. That doesn't mean privacy concerns aren't real, but it does mean AI isn't an all-knowing eye watching everything a teenager does online. Another misconception is that one "wrong click" or missed email can ruin chances forever. The systems may track patterns, but they are not waiting to punish minor, everyday mistakes.

At the same time, it is equally misleading to pretend that AI is just a neutral helper with no impact on outcomes. The models do influence who gets attention, and they can unintentionally reflect biases in the data they're trained on. Families who assume "the system will figure it out" without any thought from their side miss an opportunity to be intentional. The sweet spot is understanding AI well enough to avoid panic on one side and passivity on the other.

1.8 Why Understanding AI Is Now Part of Being "Prepared."

A generation ago, being prepared for college mainly meant knowing your GPA, test scores, and deadlines. Today, being prepared also includes understanding how technology shapes the pathway into college. You don't have to become an expert in programming or statistics. Still, you do need a working grasp of how AI influences recruitment, outreach, and, in some cases, the evaluation and organization of applications. This knowledge helps you avoid unforced errors and gives you a language for asking fair questions of schools.

For students, that might mean recognizing that the way you interact with a college's digital tools sends signals about your interest and fit. For parents, it means knowing enough to ask admissions officers, "How do you use data and AI in your recruitment process?" and listening carefully to the answer. If a college is transparent and thoughtful about its use of technology, that can increase your confidence in sending your student there. If the answer is vague or dismissive, it may be a sign to ask more questions or look elsewhere.

Ultimately, understanding AI in college recruitment is not about chasing every new app or trend. It's about recognizing that you are already inside an AI-shaped system, whether you like it or not. Learning the basics of how that system works allows your family to navigate it with more control and less fear. It turns AI from a mysterious force operating on you into a tool you can respond to, question, and sometimes even use to your advantage.

1.9 Using AI as a Trusted Assistant, Not a Shortcut

As you move deeper into this book, you'll see a recurring theme: AI should act as a **trusted** assistant, not a substitute for your own thinking, effort, or voice. The same tools that colleges use to understand you more quickly are available, in different forms, to help you understand colleges and manage the process more wisely. The key is how you use them. When families treat AI as a coach—helping brainstorm questions, organize information, and avoid mistakes—they usually feel more confident and less overwhelmed.

The trouble starts when AI becomes a shortcut that replaces real engagement. If a student uses an AI tool to write an essay from scratch, they not only risk crossing ethical lines but also lose an important chance to discover and express their own story. If a parent uses AI to manage every piece of communication while the student remains passive, the college may sense that the teenager is not ready to own their journey. AI can make tasks easier, but it cannot—and should not—replace maturity, curiosity, and effort.

Throughout the chapters ahead, we will walk through specific, ethical ways students and parents can use AI to stay organized, research schools, prepare questions, and refine their applications without handing over control. You will see practical examples of how to turn AI into a mirror that reflects your thinking to you more clearly, rather than a mask that hides who you really are. Understanding this distinction early will help you make wise choices as the pressure of junior and senior year ramps up.

1.10 Checklist for Action: Students

These actions are meant to be small, doable steps that help you start strong in an AI-shaped recruitment world. You don't need to do all of them at once; choose one or two to begin.

- Map your current digital trail.
  Take ten minutes to list where colleges might already see your activity (college search sites, university portals, test score sends) so you understand what signals you might already be sending.
- Choose three colleges to engage with intentionally.
  Pick a small set of schools that genuinely interest you and make a plan to visit their websites, sign up for information, or attend at least one event, so your interest shows up clearly.
- Create a separate, professional email for college communication.
  Use an address with your name (not nicknames or

jokes) and check it regularly, so you don't miss important messages or look unprepared when systems log your responses.

- Scan your inbox for "missed chances."
  Look back at the last month's emails from colleges and mark any that invite you to events, webinars, or special programs so you can decide which ones align with your interests.
- Start a simple "college signals" notebook or document.
  Keep track of where you filled out forms, attended sessions, or contacted reps; this makes it easier to remember who you engaged with and to build on those connections later.
- Try one AI tool as a planner, not a writer.
  Use an AI assistant to help you build a calendar of junior- or senior-year tasks or to brainstorm questions to ask colleges, while keeping your own words and decisions at the center.

1.11 Checklist for Action: Parents

These steps help you support your student without taking over or turning AI into another source of stress. Pick one area where your student seems most unsure and begin there.

- Ask how your student currently hears from colleges.
  Have a short, nonjudgmental conversation about where emails, texts, and portal messages are going so you both know what systems are already in play.

- Help set up healthy email and notification habits.
  Work together to adjust notification settings or create folders so important college messages don't get lost in promotions or social updates.
- Practice one "AI-aware" question for college reps.
  The next time you attend a college event, be ready to ask, "How does your college use data and technology in recruitment?" to open a transparent conversation.
- Encourage engagement over volume.
  Gently steer your student toward deeper involvement with a reasonable number of schools instead of pushing for a long list of applications with minimal interaction.
- Model curiosity, not fear, about AI.
  Share what you're learning from this book, admit what you don't understand yet, and invite your student to explore answers with you, so AI feels like a shared topic, not a secret weapon.
- Set boundaries for your own involvement.
  Decide where you will use tools (for research and organization) and where you will step back (essay content and personal voice), so your student can grow into ownership of the process.

2 How Colleges Use AI Behind the Scenes

2.1 A Day in the Life of an AI-Enabled Admissions Office

Picture a Tuesday morning in October—the admissions team logs in from offices, kitchen tables, and student centers across campus. Instead of starting with a blank to-do list, each counselor opens a dashboard that shows a list of "students to contact today," ranked not alphabetically, but by how likely they are to respond, apply, and enroll. The list updates in real time as students open emails, click links, or sign up for virtual events.

At the same time, a separate dashboard shows how many seats are still open in specific majors, which regions are under-represented in this year's applicant pool, and where financial aid budgets are running tight. None of this information appears magically. Under the hood, AI systems are constantly analyzing streams of data—from test score sends and inquiry forms to web behavior and event registrations—and turning them into recommendations for the people who sit in those admissions seats. Humans still make the decisions. The machines shape the menu.

2.2 The Core Tools: CRMs, Predictive Models, and Chatbots

When people hear "AI," they often think of robots or sci-fi movies. In college recruitment, AI mostly lives within tools named "enrollment CRM," "student success platform," or "communications system." At the heart of many admissions offices is a Customer Relationship Management system—essentially a large, specialized address book that stores every interaction with prospective students. Over time, these systems have evolved from simple databases into smart platforms that can score students, suggest next steps, and automate messages based on behavior.

Layered on top of the CRM are predictive models—statistical and machine learning tools that estimate things like "likelihood to apply," "likelihood to enroll," or "likelihood to need extra support." These models look at patterns in past data (who applied, who enrolled, who graduated) and use them to make educated guesses about current prospects. Then there are chatbots and virtual assistants on college websites. Some are basic rule-based tools; others use generative AI to answer open-ended questions, guide students through forms, and escalate complicated issues to human staff when they get stuck.

For students, all of this can blur together. You might chat with a bot at 11:30 p.m., get a personalized email at 7:00 a.m., and see your portal recommend a major based on your interests. Behind the scenes, these tools share data. The key point is that they are connected: information doesn't live in one place anymore. When used thoughtfully, that connection can make the process smoother; when used carelessly, it can make the system feel overwhelming or intrusive.

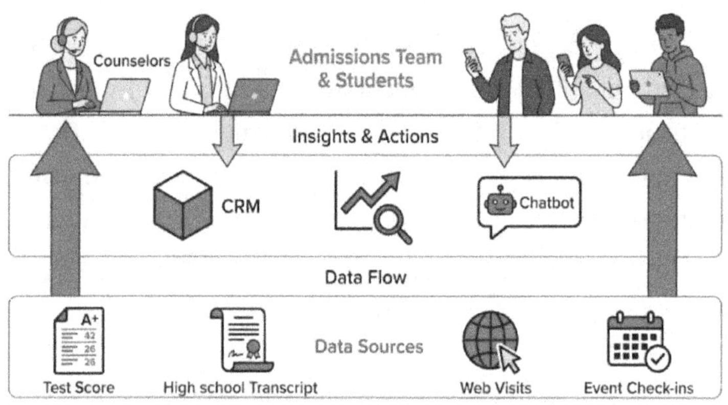

2.3 Where the Data Comes From

To understand how colleges use AI, you need to understand where the data feeding those systems comes from. Some sources are obvious. When you fill out an online inquiry form, register for a visit, or submit a test score, you are clearly providing information. Your high school also sends data when you ask them to transmit your transcript or when they upload information to common platforms. Many colleges purchase lists from testing organizations or national search services that include basic details about your academic profile and interests.

Other data sources are less visible but still important. When you click a link in an email from a college, the system can record that click. When you spend time on certain pages of a university website, analytics tools can track the approximate time on the page and which sections you viewed. If you interact with the college through a third-party platform—like a college search website—those interactions can sometimes be shared with the institution, depending on the agreements in place. Taken together, these touchpoints create a timeline of your engagement.

For parents, this can raise valid questions. It's natural to ask, "How much do they know about my child?" and "Are they allowed to collect all of this?" The answer is that colleges are generally working within privacy laws and contracts, but they are also using every legal tool available to meet their enrollment goals. That's why families need to read consent language on forms, understand which services are sharing data, and be intentional about where and how they engage.

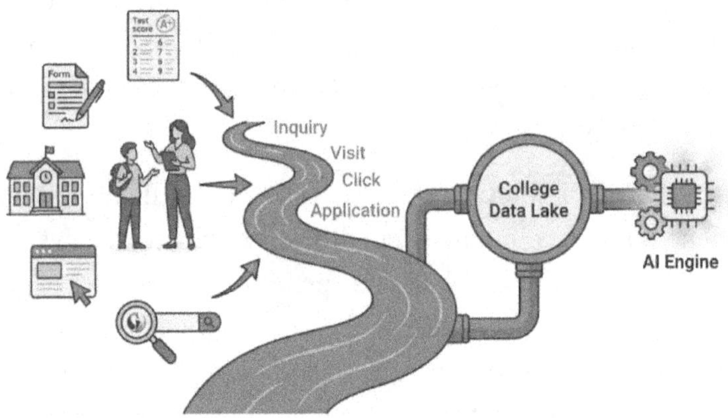

2.4 What These Systems Actually Do with the Data

Once data arrives in the college's systems, AI tools start doing three main things: sorting, scoring, and suggesting. First, sorting. AI helps organize large numbers of students into more manageable groups—by geography, academic interest, engagement level, or potential financial need. Instead of manually scanning thousands of records, a counselor can click "students interested in nursing within 100 miles who attended last week's webinar" and instantly see a focused list.

Second, scoring. Predictive models assign scores—usually numbers that never appear on your screen—such as "likelihood to apply" or "likelihood to enroll if admitted." These scores don't guarantee anything, but they influence how often a student hears from the college and how much human attention their record receives. A student with a high "likelihood to enroll" score might get a personal phone call and a targeted scholarship offer; a student with a lower score might receive more general communication.

Third, suggesting. AI tools propose "next best actions" for the admissions team: send a text reminder, invite to a major-specific event, or prompt a counselor to follow up after a campus visit. In some cases, the system might even suggest who on the team is best to reach out to—perhaps pairing a first-generation student with a counselor who also shares that background. None of this replaces application review, but it shapes which relationships are cultivated before and after the application arrives.

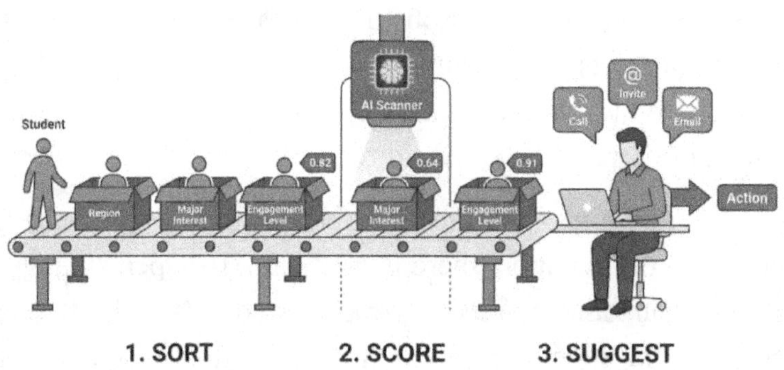

2.5 How Predictive Analytics Shapes Recruitment Strategy

To appreciate how deeply AI affects recruitment, imagine a college planning its travel schedule for the fall. In the past, staff might return to the same high schools they had always visited. Now, predictive analytics can show where past visits actually turned into applications and enrollments. A model might reveal that visiting one particular school in a rural area leads to a small number of applicants but a very high enrollment rate, while visiting another school produces many inquiries but almost no eventual students. Those patterns can shift where the college sends its limited staff and dollars.

AI also influences which programs get extra promotion. If a model predicts that interest in computer science is surging while spots are limited, the college might be more cautious in outreach to borderline students for that major, or it might highlight related programs like data science or information systems. Conversely, if a humanities department has capacity, the system may suggest emphasizing communications majors to students who show related interests. The result is a recruitment plan that is less about "we always do it this way" and more about "this is where the data says we should focus."

For families, this means that behind every email, postcard, or invitation, there is often an AI-shaped strategy. When your student receives repeated outreach from one college and silence from another, it is rarely random. It reflects how those institutions assess the odds of successfully recruiting your student, given their goals, budgets, and capacity. That doesn't mean they are perfectly accurate—but it does mean their actions are influenced by patterns that most families never see.

AI-GUIDED STRATEGY, HUMAN CHOICE

2.6 The Invisible Hand in Communications: Automation and Personalization

If you've ever wondered how a college has time to send you an email that mentions your intended major, your state, and the specific event you attended, the answer is almost always automation plus personalization. AI-enabled systems let colleges create content-building blocks—introductions, major-specific paragraphs, location references, and event follow-ups—and then assemble them into different combinations tailored to each student's profile and behavior. The message you receive feels like it was written just for you, because in a way, it was assembled just for you.

These systems also decide timing and frequency. An AI model might learn that students like you are more likely to open emails on Sunday evening, or that texting is especially effective for last-minute reminders about events. Over time, the system finetunes not only what you receive but when you receive it. For some students, this can feel pleasantly attentive. For others, it can feel like too much. Parents often see their students' phones lighting up with messages and worry: "Are they being pressured?" or "Is this just spam with better marketing?"

The deeper truth is that these communication patterns are rarely random. They are the result of constant testing—A/B experiments comparing subject lines, send times, and message formats. AI watches which messages get opened and which get ignored, then quietly shifts strategy. That's why students need to recognize that their responses, including deleting or ignoring messages, become part of the college's learning loop. Engaging thoughtfully instead of reflexively gives you more control over how these systems perceive your interest.

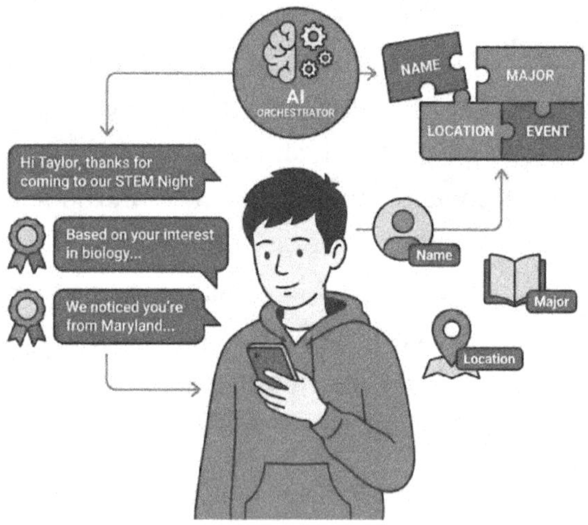

2.7 Parents' View from the Kitchen Table

From the parent side, much of this activity shows up as cluttered inboxes and a steady stream of notifications. You may see messages addressed to your student that seem warm and personal, and you may also receive copies or separate messages intended for you. It can be confusing to distinguish which communications are truly individualized and which are automated, especially when you're trying to decide how seriously to take a financial aid estimate or an invitation to a "special program."

One practical way to think about it is this: the personalization in the message (using your student's name, interests, or location) is often generated automatically, but the decision to deploy that campaign to a specific group of students usually comes from a collaboration between AI and human staff. That means there is intent behind what you see, even if a robot assembled the sentences. When you read a message, it helps to ask, "What is this college trying to learn about us or encourage us to do right now?" Are they gauging interest in a major, testing whether an event format works, or assessing price sensitivity through scholarship offers?

As a parent, you have a unique vantage point. You can step back from the flood of messages and help your student interpret patterns: Which colleges are consistent in their communication? Which messages feel aligned with your student's goals, and which feel like generic sales pitches? Instead of treating every message as urgent, you can help your student sort communications into categories—

informational, relationship-building, or transactional—so that AI-driven outreach becomes one input among many, not the primary driver of decisions.

2.8 How Chatbots and Virtual Assistants Fit In

Many colleges now place chatbots on their websites and portals to answer questions around the clock. Some are straightforward: they recognize specific phrases and route you to FAQs or forms. Others use more advanced AI, allowing you to type "I'm worried about affording this school" and receive a sequence of follow-up questions and links that feel conversational. For students who are hesitant to call an office or who are researching late at night, these tools can be genuinely helpful.

Behind the scenes, chatbots also generate valuable data for the college. They log the questions students ask most often, the points where conversations stall, and the links that people actually click. AI models can analyze those logs to improve responses over time or flag topics that need more human attention—such as confusing financial aid language or unclear housing policies. In some systems, when a conversation reaches a certain level of complexity or emotional intensity, the bot will escalate to a human counselor, often with a summary of what has already been discussed.

For families, the main thing to remember is that chatbots are assistants, not authorities. They are trained on whatever information they have been given, which may be incomplete, out of date, or overly general. It's wise to use bots for basic questions—deadlines, forms, where to find resources—and to treat answers about money, special circumstances, or policy appeals as starting points, not final decisions. Teaching your student when to move from a chat window to a live human conversation is one of the most useful skills you can pass along in this AI-enabled landscape.

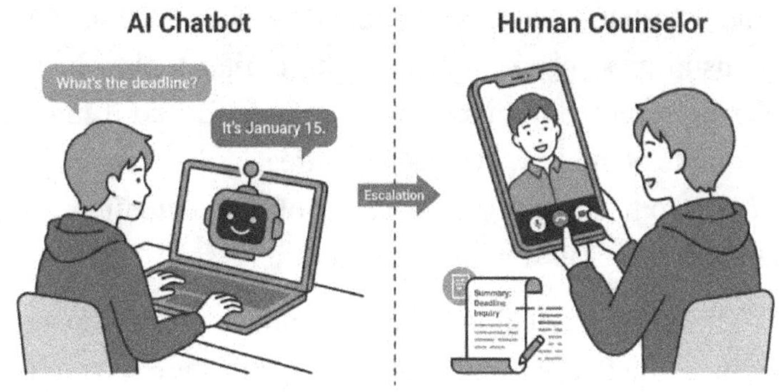

2.9 Benefits and Risks: A Balanced View

It's easy to see AI in college recruitment as either a miracle or a menace. The truth is more balanced. On the plus side, AI allows colleges to reach students in places they might never have visited physically. It can surface first-- or lower-income students whose engagement patterns show strong interest and resilience, even if their schools don't have a long history of sending graduates to four-year colleges. AI can also streamline communications so that students receive more relevant information and fewer one-size-fits-all brochures.

On the risk side, AI systems are only as fair and accurate as the data and instructions they receive. If past recruitment focused heavily on certain regions or schools, predictive models may continue that pattern unless someone deliberately corrects it. Students who don't or can't engage online as often—because of limited internet access, family responsibilities, or skepticism about digital tools—may be under-represented in this data-driven world. And if families don't understand how AI shapes outreach, they can misread silence from a college as rejection, or attention as a guarantee of admission or generous aid.

The purpose of this chapter is not to scare you or to convince you that AI will determine your future. It is to pull back the curtain so you know what's happening behind the scenes. When you understand both the benefits and the risks, you are in a better position to use AI-driven tools wisely, to ask good questions of colleges, and to make decisions based on your own values rather than on what an algorithm predicts you might do.

2.10 Using AI as a Trusted Assistant in This Stage

Knowing that colleges use AI behind the scenes also opens the door for you to use AI tools on your side of the table. At this stage of the process—researching, exploring, and responding to outreach—AI can serve as a coach to help you stay organized and make sense of the noise. For example, a student might use an AI assistant to summarize a long financial aid email into key bullet points to discuss with a parent, or to generate a list of clarifying questions to ask a college representative at an upcoming webinar. The student still decides what to ask and what matters most. The AI helps structure the information.

Parents can use AI in similar ways. You might paste in information from several colleges' websites and ask an AI assistant to highlight differences in housing policies, support services, or payment plans. You can then bring that digest to a family discussion, rather than expecting your student to read every word on their own. The critical boundary is that AI should help you understand and compare what colleges are offering; it should not fill out forms for you, invent personal stories, or pretend to be you or your student in communications with schools.

By consciously choosing assistant-type tasks for AI—organizing, summarizing, planning—you keep the heart of decision-making where it belongs: with your family. You become more capable, not more replaceable. When students and parents work together this way, they're better prepared to push back gently if a college's AI-driven outreach feels too aggressive or confusing, and to affirm their own priorities even when the algorithms suggest otherwise.

2.11 Checklist for Action: Students

- Identify which college tools are using AI.
  Make a quick list of where you see automation—chatbots, personalized emails, suggested majors—

so you can recognize when algorithms are likely shaping your experience.

- Track your meaningful engagement, not just clicks. Start a simple log of the events you attend, the questions you ask, and the conversations you have with counselors, so you remember real connections beyond what the system measures.
- Use a chatbot for practice questions.
  Before emailing a real counselor, test your basic questions (deadlines, forms, locations) with a college chatbot so you can save human time for deeper, more personal issues.
- Try an AI assistant to summarize college info.
  When you receive a long email or find a dense web page, paste the text into an AI tool and ask for a summary to help you understand what's important before you decide what to do.
- Notice how different colleges communicate.
  Over a month, pay attention to which schools send thoughtful, helpful messages versus constant generic reminders, and use that insight to refine your college list.

2.12 Checklist for Action: Parents

- Ask your student where AI is showing up.
  Have a calm conversation about chatbots, recommendation tools, and personalized emails they've seen, so you can talk about how those tools might be influencing their feelings.

- Help your student build a "college communication hub."
  Create a shared folder or document to organize key emails, links, and portal logins, reducing stress and making AI-driven outreach easier to manage.
- Use AI to translate "admissions language" into plain language.
  When you encounter confusing financial aid or policy text, use an AI assistant to rephrase it more simply, then double-check details directly with the college when needed.
- Model healthy skepticism without fear.
  When you receive a polished, personalized message, talk with your student about what is likely automated and what might reflect genuine human interest, so they learn to read between the lines.
- Prepare one or two questions about AI for info sessions.
  For example, "How do you use data and technology in recruitment and advising?" Practice asking this so you feel comfortable bringing it up with admissions staff in person or online.

3 The Rise of Algorithmic Student Profiling

3.1 Two Juniors, Two Very Different Digital Shadows

Imagine two juniors at the same high school. Jordan spends evenings on college websites, clicking through majors, watching student-life videos, and signing up for virtual tours with a few schools that really stand out. Their email inbox shows a mix of confirmations, reminders, and follow-ups. Jordan doesn't post much on social media, but when a college invites them to an info session, they usually say yes.

Alex, on the other hand, hears about colleges mostly from friends and teachers. They Google schools, read a few pages, maybe watch a video, and then move on without signing up for anything. They use a personal email account that's overflowing with promotions, and many college messages get lost. On social media, Alex posts actively about community projects and leadership roles—but never tags colleges or follows admissions accounts. On the surface, Jordan and Alex are both strong students. Behind the scenes, though, the digital record colleges see looks very different. One shows up as a series of clear signals. The other shows up as scattered traces.

3.2 What "Algorithmic Student Profiling" Really Means

"Profiling" is a loaded word, especially for families who have experienced bias in other systems. In the college recruitment context, algorithmic student profiling usually means using AI to build and update a digital picture of each prospective student based on available data. The goal, from the college's perspective, is to understand who might be a good fit, who is most likely to enroll, and what support each student might need. But the way that picture is built—and what it includes—matters.

At a basic level, an AI-driven profile pulls together things like academic indicators (grades, courses, test scores if submitted), school context, and engagement signals (website visits, event attendance, email interactions). Some systems also incorporate broader data, such as estimated financial capacity or first-generation status, based on information students or high schools provide. The profile is not a single number; it's more like a structured file that AI models use to make predictions and recommendations. Over time, each new interaction updates the profile, much like adding brushstrokes to a portrait.

For students and parents, the key is to understand that this portrait is not neutral. It reflects what data is collected, how it is interpreted, and which behaviors the system "likes" or rewards. A student who is deeply engaged offline but barely visible online may have a thinner profile than their true potential warrants. Conversely, a student who clicks everything without much thought may appear highly engaged even if they are undecided. Recognizing this gap between real life and digital picture is the first step to managing your presence strategically.

3.3 The Ingredients of a Digital Profile

Different colleges and vendors use different recipes, but many algorithmic profiles draw from similar categories of information. You can think of them as ingredients in a dish; change the mix, and you change the outcome. Common ingredients include:

- Academic record
  This covers your coursework, grades, class rigor, and sometimes test scores, painting a picture of your preparation for college-level work.
- School and community context
  Data about your high school, such as size, past outcomes, and available courses, can help colleges interpret your achievements in context.
- Engagement behavior
  Actions like opening emails, attending events, visiting web pages, and using portals signal interest and help AI gauge your connection to the college.
- Stated interests and goals
  Majors you select on forms, clubs you mention, and survey responses about your goals help shape how colleges imagine your fit with programs.
- Demographic and background information
  When shared, factors such as geography, first-generation status, and, sometimes, race/ethnicity inform both outreach and, in some cases, efforts to support equity and diversity.

Not every college uses all these categories, and not every category is weighted equally. But together, they influence which students are tagged as "likely to apply," "likely to enroll," or "needs more information," and which students receive extra attention, scholarship outreach, or specialized messaging.

3.4 How Algorithms Group and Label Students

Once profiles exist, AI systems start grouping students into segments. These segments might have internal names like "High-Engagement STEM Explorers," "Price-Sensitive In-State Students," or "First-Gen Urban Leaders." Admissions staff use these segments to tailor messages, decide who receives personal calls, and prioritize travel or virtual programming. The segmentation itself is algorithmic, based on patterns in past data—who applied, who enrolled, who graduated successfully.

Within each segment, students may be assigned scores that indicate the model's estimate of their likelihood of taking specific actions. These scores are often invisible to families, but they strongly influence where the college invests time and money. A high score might lead to extra outreach or a targeted scholarship campaign. A low score might mean a student receives only standard communications, even if they thrive at the school. Importantly, these scores are predictions, not verdicts. They can be wrong, especially for students whose backgrounds or behaviors differ from the majority in the training data.

This is why relying blindly on segments and scores can be risky for colleges and frustrating for families. If the model has learned patterns that reflect historical inequities—like under-recruiting students from certain neighborhoods or under-estimating students from underfunded schools—it may continue those patterns unless someone deliberately questions the results. Families don't need to see the code, but they do benefit from knowing that these systems exist and asking colleges how they check for fairness in their profiling and segmentation.

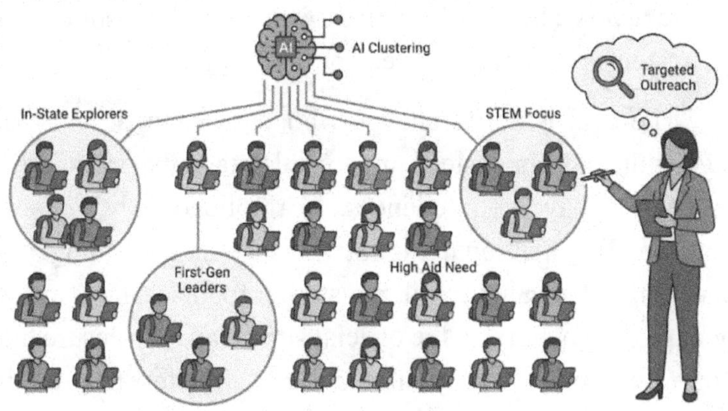

3.5 When Your Online Behavior Speaks Louder Than Your Voice

In an AI-driven recruitment world, your online behavior can sometimes speak louder than statements you make in essays or conversations—at least early in the process. If a system sees that you repeatedly explore certain majors, attend related events, and open specific message types, it infers genuine interest. If you rarely engage, it may indicate you're not serious about the school, even if you quietly care a lot but feel overwhelmed, shy, or skeptical of marketing.

This dynamic can be especially tricky for students who are more private online or who share devices with family members. For example, if a sibling clicks a college email link on a shared computer, that activity might be linked to the wrong student profile. If a student accesses college websites mostly from school computers, security filters might block tracking scripts, making engagement look lighter than it is. And for students with limited internet access, every click is a sacrifice of time or data—something AI systems don't always "see" or honor.

The goal is not to change who you are to fit what the algorithm expects. Instead, it's to understand that silence and invisibility have consequences. If a college truly interests you, small, intentional digital actions—like creating and checking a dedicated email, registering for at least one event, or exploring majors on the official site—can help ensure that your interest shows up in the same systems that might otherwise overlook you. You're not performing for a machine; you're making sure the parts of your story you care about have a chance to be seen.

Behavior vs. Words in Early AI Systems

3.6 Equity, Bias, and Uneven Visibility

Algorithmic profiling doesn't happen in a vacuum; it sits atop social and educational systems that are already unequal. If a model is trained mostly on data from students who had stable internet access, supportive counselors, and families familiar with college, it may learn patterns that work well for those students and poorly for others. For example, it might assume that students who attend multiple virtual events are more likely to enroll, without considering that some students can't attend due to work, caregiving, or technology limits.

Bias can enter in subtle ways. A model might over-weight test scores because previous classes relied heavily on them, under-estimating students whose strengths show up better in recommendations, portfolios, or interviews. It might expect certain engagement patterns from students in specific zip codes, using geography as a rough indicator of income or school quality. Even if the model never sees race directly, these proxies can reinforce racial and economic disparities. Colleges that care about fairness must deliberately test their models for different groups and adjust when patterns look skewed.

For families, this raises important questions to bring to admissions officers. You are within your rights to ask how the institution monitors its AI tools for bias, whether they consider first-generation or low-income status in ways that expand opportunity, and how they make sure students without strong digital footprints still get considered fully. You may not receive technical details, but an honest, thoughtful answer tells you a lot about whether the college sees students as more than data points.

3.7 Student Story: Mary and the "Invisible" Leadership

Consider Mary, a junior who spends most afternoons caring for younger siblings while her parents work. She doesn't attend many online events because evenings are hectic, and the family's internet connection is shared and slow. Her school doesn't host frequent college fairs. Still, she has built a strong record of leadership—organizing food drives through her church, advocating for safer crosswalks in her neighborhood, and mentoring ninth-graders informally. None of those activities automatically shows up in the college's engagement data.

On paper, Mary's academic profile is solid, and her teacher recommendations are enthusiastic. But in the world of AI-driven recruitment, she may appear less "invested" than peers who can easily attend multiple virtual tours and check their email constantly. If a college relies heavily on engagement scores to prioritize outreach, Maya might receive fewer touches, fewer personalized opportunities, or less information about scholarships designed for students exactly like her. Her leadership is real; her digital shadow is faint.

Mary's story (and stories like hers) highlight why understanding algorithmic profiling matters. If Mary and her family know that online engagement influences how colleges see her, they can make a few targeted moves—attending at least one virtual event, responding thoughtfully to key emails, or connecting with a regional rep—to ensure she doesn't disappear into the background. At the same time, colleges that hear stories like Mary's can adjust their systems to value context, not just clicks, and to build pathways that don't penalize students who carry heavy responsibilities at home.

AI needs human context to see the full picture.

3.8 Parent Story: Mr. and Mrs. Smith and the Data Trail They Didn't Expect

Mr. and Mrs. Smith both did not attend four-year colleges, and the admissions landscape feels unfamiliar. They are careful about privacy and have always told their daughter Sofia not to share too much online. When Sofia starts receiving targeted messages from colleges referencing her intended major and interests, her parents are surprised. "We never told them that," they think. "How do they know?" First, the messages feel helpful. Over time, the volume grows, and the Riveras start to worry that invisible systems are predicting more about their child than they understand.

During a virtual parent session, they decide to ask a direct question: "What data do you collect about our students, and how do you use it?" The admissions representative explains that when Sofia used online college search tools, filled out forms, and clicked certain pages, those actions were recorded and shared in accordance with privacy agreements. Sofia's interest in biology and healthcare stemmed from surveys she completed and the content she viewed. The representative acknowledges that the tools use AI to recommend resources and plan outreach but emphasizes that people still make final admissions decisions.

This conversation doesn't erase the Smiths' concerns, but it gives them language and confidence. They start reading consent statements more carefully, discussing with Sofia which platforms to use, and encouraging her to take charge of her digital trail rather than leaving everything on autopilot. They also learn that they can opt out of some communication or adjust preferences, reducing noise while preserving essential messages. Their story shows how parents can move from feeling watched to feeling informed and proactive, without pretending AI isn't part of the picture.

3.9 Practical Guardrails Families Can Set for Themselves

While you can't control how every college builds its models, you can set practical guardrails for your own digital behavior. Think of these as family-level policies for living in an AI-driven admissions world. One guardrail might be, "We don't share social security numbers or detailed financial information anywhere except secure, official application portals." Another might be, "We're comfortable with Sofia using official college and nonprofit search tools, but we'll read their privacy policies together before she opts in." Having these rules written down turns vague worry into clear boundaries.

You can also set guardrails around time and attention. For example, agree that you'll batch-process college emails twice a week instead of reacting to every notification, so the AI systems don't condition you into constant urgency. Decide that for any major decision—choosing a college list, responding to an offer, drafting an essay, using AI assistants only for planning, organizing, and brainstorming, not for writing the final text or making choices for you. This keeps control in human hands and reduces the risk of over-sharing sensitive information with tools you don't fully understand.

By building your own guardrails, you teach your student a skill that will matter long after admissions: how to live thoughtfully in systems that watch, sort, and predict. You can't opt out of every algorithm, but you can choose how you show up in them, how much power you give their predictions over your decisions, and how you advocate for fairness when you see gaps. In that sense, algorithmic profiling becomes not just a challenge to navigate, but a chance to practice digital citizenship as a family.

3.10 Checklist for Action: Students

- Make your "real story" visible in official channels. Identify one or two colleges you care about and be sure your leadership, responsibilities, and interests show up in forms, activity lists, or conversations—not just on social media.
- Choose 2–3 meaningful online interactions per school.
  For colleges you like, aim for a small number of purposeful engagements (an event, a webinar question, a major exploration) instead of dozens of random clicks.
- Review your college emails and portals weekly. Set a time to log in, open key messages, and respond where it matters so your digital profile reflects real interest, and you don't miss opportunities hidden in the noise.
- Use AI to help describe, not invent, your activities. Ask an AI assistant to help you organize and phrase your real responsibilities and achievements more clearly, but ensure the content is true to your experiences and in your own voice.
- Write down how you want colleges to see you. Create a short personal definition (three to five traits or themes) you want your digital activity to reflect, and use it to guide where you sign up, what you click, and how you respond.

3.11 Checklist for Action: Parents

- Talk through the idea of a "digital profile" with your student.
  Use plain language to explain that colleges see patterns in behavior, then ask your student how they feel about that and where they want to be more intentional.
- Help your student map their offline strengths to online signals.
  List leadership, caregiving, work, or community roles they hold, then brainstorm ways those can appear in applications, forms, or appropriate online spaces colleges will actually see.
- Set privacy and sharing boundaries.
  Decide which platforms and forms you trust, what information you'll never share except in official applications, and how you'll evaluate new tools before using them.
- Prepare two fairness questions to ask colleges.
  For example, "How do you make sure your data and AI tools don't overlook students from under-resourced schools?" Practice asking so you feel comfortable raising it in sessions.
- Model calm, curious engagement with AI.
  When you hear about algorithmic profiling, avoid either panic or dismissal. Instead, share what you're learning, ask your student what they notice, and show that you're willing to adapt without losing your values.

4 Personalized Outreach: When AI Knows You Better Than You Think

4.1 "How Did They Know That?"

It usually starts with a subject line that makes you pause. Maybe it's "Taylor, three things every future engineer should know," arriving the day after you spent twenty minutes reading about engineering majors. Or it's "A note for families from Prince George's County," right after you filled out a form with your home ZIP code. No one from that college has called your house. You've never had a one-on-one conversation. And yet, the email sounds as if it were written just for you.

Parents often tell me this is the moment they realize something has changed. In their own admissions experience, messages from colleges were broad and generic. Now, their students' inboxes are full of messages that mention specific majors, interests, and even concerns such as financial aid or being the first in their family to go to college. It feels like someone is reading over your shoulder. What's happening is that AI-powered systems are stitching together pieces of information you've already shared—directly or indirectly—and turning them into what looks like individual attention at scale.

4.2 From Mass Mail to "Just for You."

Before AI-driven systems became common, colleges sent what we now call "spray and pray" messages. They bought large lists of names and blasted out the same brochure or email to everyone. Students received piles of mail that all sounded alike. It was easy to tune out, and it was hard for colleges to tell who genuinely cared. As competition for students grew—and as budgets tightened, schools needed a smarter way to communicate, one that didn't waste resources or students' patience.

AI made that shift possible by learning from patterns. Instead of sending the same message to 20,000 students, the system can now divide that list into hundreds of smaller groups based on interests, behavior, and background. One group might receive stories about campus research in biology, another might see highlights from the business school, and a third might get messages about support for first-generation students. Within each group, the system can still insert individual details, such as your name and location, but the real power lies in matching the message's theme to what the AI believes you care about.

For students, this can feel flattering—“They really see me!”—or overwhelming—“Why are they in my head?” For parents, it can feel both efficient and manipulative. Both reactions are understandable. The important thing to remember is that this kind of personalization is based on data you’ve already provided or actions you’ve already taken. The system isn’t reading your mind; it’s connecting dots that used to sit in separate files.

4.3 What Signals Fuel Personalized Outreach

To understand how personalization works, it helps to know what kinds of signals colleges actually use. Some are obvious. When you choose an intended major on a form or click “Interested in nursing?” in a survey, that information feeds directly into the system. When you register for a virtual event about engineering, the system learns that this topic deserves a spot in your future messages. When you identify as first-generation, in-state, or commuter-interested, that, too, becomes part of the picture.

Other signals are quieter but still important. The system pays attention to which emails you open and ignore, which links you click, and how often you log in to your portal. If you consistently open messages about student life but rarely click on athletic updates, the AI may emphasize campus culture in future emails. If you keep revisiting the cost and financial aid page, the system may prioritize sending you clearer information about scholarships, payment plans, or net price calculators. Over time, these signals create a feedback loop—the more you interact, the more precisely the system "tunes" its outreach.

From the college's perspective, this is helpful. They don't want to waste your time with irrelevant information. From your point of view, it's important to realize that you play a role in training the system. Every click, open, and registration teaches the AI what "people like you" respond to. That doesn't mean you should overthink every action, but it does mean being intentional: if a topic genuinely matters to you, it's worth engaging with those messages; if it doesn't, don't let the algorithm decide your interests for you.

AI Tuning Content Mix based on Student Signals

4.4 When Personalization Starts to Feel Like Pressure

There's a fine line between feeling seen and feeling targeted. Some students tell me that personalized messages motivate them—they feel encouraged when a college notices their interests and follows up with relevant opportunities. Others describe feeling like they're in a constant sales funnel, especially when messages use urgency ("Last chance!" "Don't miss out!") or when they receive more reminders than they can reasonably respond to. Parents may worry that this pressure is nudging decisions before the family has had a chance to talk things through.

AI systems are good at spotting what has worked in the past to drive actions—like clicking "Apply Now" or registering for a campus visit. If a countdown timer in an email leads more students to sign up for an event, the system will suggest using that tactic again. If repeated messages about a scholarship drive more inquiries, those campaigns may become more aggressive. What the AI can't see is the stress this sometimes causes, or that "more" attention isn't always a "better" fit. That's where your human judgment comes in.

It's perfectly reasonable to set boundaries. You can unsubscribe from non-essential lists, adjust notification settings, or, as a family, decide to treat certain messages as informational rather than urgent. You can also pay attention to how each college communicates under pressure: do they respect your time and choices, or do they rely heavily on fear of missing out? Those patterns tell you something about the school's culture, not just about its technology.

4.5 Turning Personalized Outreach into a Two-Way Conversation

One of the most powerful things students can do in this environment is to treat personalized outreach not as a one-way broadcast, but as the beginning of a conversation. If an email about a particular major catch your attention, reply with a question that actually matters to you: "Can you tell me how students in this program find internships?" or

“What kind of support is there for someone changing majors?” Those replies often go to real people, and they can shift you from being a data point in a segment to being a student a counselor remembers.

Parents can join this conversation thoughtfully. When colleges send messages directed at families, especially about cost, support services, or first-generation resources, you can respond with specific concerns rather than just reading passively. Asking, “How do you support students who need to work part-time?” or “What does communication with families look like once our student enrolls?” invites a human answer that goes beyond any algorithmic script. It also signals that your family is engaged, values clarity, and is thinking seriously about fit.

The key is to keep your voice authentic. You don’t need to sound like a brochure or try to impress a chatbot. You do, however, want to make sure that when personalization opens a door, you walk through it with real questions and honest information. AI can bring opportunities to your screen. Only you can decide which ones deserve your energy and how you want colleges to know you beyond their predictions.

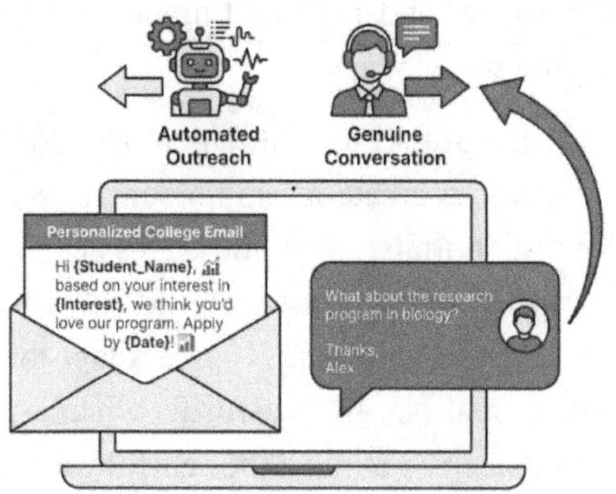

4.6 Using AI on Your Side to Decode and Organize Outreach

The same technologies colleges use to personalize outreach can help you manage it. Instead of trying to read every message in real time, students can use an AI assistant as a kind of "filter and explainer." For example, you might paste two or three important emails from different colleges into an AI tool and ask, "Summarize the key points and deadlines in plain language." That doesn't replace your responsibility to read carefully, but it helps you make sense of long, jargon-heavy messages more quickly.

Parents can do something similar with financial and policy information. If cost letters or scholarship offers feel confusing, you can use an AI assistant to outline what each college seems to be offering, what's guaranteed, and what depends on future conditions. You would still confirm details directly with the school's financial aid office—but you're starting from a clearer, more organized place. This is exactly the kind of "trusted assistant" role AI is good at:

sorting, comparing, and highlighting, while humans make the final judgments.

You can also use AI to draft a personal communication plan. Ask, "Help us create a simple schedule for checking college emails, portals, and messages each week," or "Generate a list of questions we should ask when a college invites us to a special program." Then adapt that plan to fit your family's reality. In a world where personalized outreach never sleeps, having a thoughtful way to respond—on your terms—turns AI from a source of stress into support for your own strategy.

4.7 Checklist for Action: Students

- Notice which messages truly help you.
  Over a week or two, pay attention to which college emails or texts give you useful information or opportunities, and which feel like noise, so you can focus your energy where it matters.
- Use your replies to show your real questions.
  When a personalized email sparks interest, reply

with one or two honest questions about programs, support, or campus life to move from automated outreach to a real conversation.

- Create a simple "inbox routine."
  Set specific days and times to check college emails and portals, and stick to them so you're responding thoughtfully rather than reacting to every notification.
- Try AI to summarize long messages—not to decide for you.
  When you get a dense email, let an AI assistant summarize it in simpler terms, then read the original carefully to confirm details and decide what actions you'll take.
- Keep a short list of your favorite messages.
  Save two or three emails that felt genuinely helpful or encouraging and use them as a reference for the tone and content you prefer when you compare colleges later.

4.8 Checklist for Action: Parents

- Clarify how often you and your student will review outreach together.
  Agree on a regular time to sit down and look at key messages, so you stay informed without hovering over every notification your student receives.
- Help your student set communication boundaries.
  Talk through when it makes sense to unsubscribe, adjust notifications, or politely say "no thanks" to

certain events or programs, so outreach doesn't feel like constant pressure.

- Use AI to decode complex financial or policy emails.
  When a college sends a detailed message about cost, aid, or deadlines, use an AI assistant to outline the main points, then verify anything important directly with the school.
- Pay attention to each college's communication style.
  Notice which schools are clear, respectful, and responsive versus those that rely heavily on urgency or hype and include that in your family's discussion of overall fit.
- Encourage your student to keep their voice at the center.
  Remind them that personalized messages are helpful tools, not orders, and that their values, goals, and well-thought-out questions matter more than any algorithm's prediction.

5 AI-Enhanced College Search Tools

5.1 When the Search Bar Becomes a Guide

Not long ago, "college search" meant stacks of guidebooks, a few bookmarked websites, and maybe a binder full of brochures. Now, many students start with a single search bar on a college-planning site or app. They type in something simple—"good pre-med schools near me" or "colleges with strong business programs and scholarships"—and instantly receive a list that feels surprisingly tailored. Rankings, location filters, and cost estimates appear in seconds. It's easy to forget that behind that clean screen, AI is doing a lot of heavy lifting.

Parents see the same shift from the sidelines. Instead of watching their teens flip through thick catalogs, they see them on their phones, scrolling through "recommended colleges," quiz results, and interactive maps. Some tools ask personality questions, others analyze interests or career goals, and within minutes, they present "matches" and "reach," "target," or "safety" schools. It can feel like magic—and it can also feel risky. If a tool's recommendations become the main driver of a student's list, an unseen algorithm may be making some of the biggest educational suggestions of their life.

5.2 What These Search Tools Actually Do

Most AI-enhanced college search tools work in two stages. First, they gather information about the student. This might include basics like GPA range, test scores (if available), preferred majors, location preferences, and size or setting (urban, suburban, rural). Some tools go further, asking about extracurricular interests, learning preferences, or potential careers. In the background, the platform also records behavior—what you click on, how long you stay on certain profiles, and which schools you mark as "favorite" or "not interested."

Second, they compare that information to a large database of colleges and past user behavior. AI models look for patterns: which schools have historically attracted students with similar profiles, where those students were admitted, and where they ultimately enrolled. Based on those patterns, the system assigns "match" levels or fit scores and orders the list accordingly. Over time, as more students use the tool, the models learn which recommendations were accurate (students applied and enrolled) and which missed the mark (students ignored or quickly removed those options). That feedback loop makes future suggestions seem smarter—but only within the patterns the tool has already experienced.

This means that AI-driven search tools are very good at steering you toward colleges that look like your established preferences and like the choices made by similar students before you. They are less good at helping you discover completely new options outside those patterns—schools in unfamiliar regions, institutions that serve non-traditional paths, or emerging programs that haven't generated much data yet. Used wisely, they can narrow an overwhelming universe of options into a manageable starting set. Used blindly, they can quietly shrink your world.

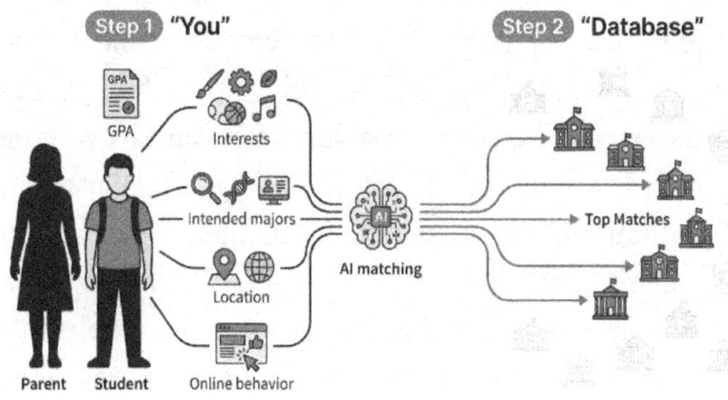

5.3 Benefits: Focus, Filters, and First Looks

For many students, AI-powered search tools provide real relief. Instead of trying to consider thousands of colleges at once, they can apply filters and instantly see schools that match basic criteria—size, location, majors, and estimated cost ranges. Some tools include early indicators of acceptance rates and typical academic profiles, helping students avoid lists filled with only extremely selective options. For first-generation students or those from under-resourced schools, these tools can offer a first structured look at what's available beyond the handful of colleges they've heard about from family and friends.

Parents often appreciate the practical features as well. Being able to compare average costs, graduation rates, or student-faculty ratios side by side gives families something concrete to discuss, especially when emotions and opinions run high. Tools that suggest "financial fit" or flag generous aid patterns can be especially helpful for families who need to balance aspiration with affordability. When used as a starting point for conversation, these platforms can bring hidden gems onto the radar—regional publics, honors programs, or smaller private colleges that genuinely fit the student's goals but don't have national name recognition.

These benefits matter. Without some structure, the search process can feel paralyzing. AI-enhanced tools can turn "I have no idea where to start" into "Here are ten schools that seem worth a closer look." The key is to remember that "first look" should not become "final verdict." The tool is offering possibilities, not a destiny.

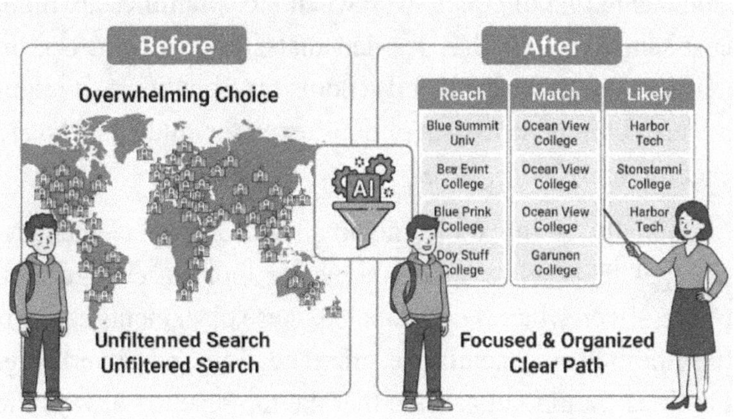

5.4 Blind Spots and Hidden Assumptions

Every AI system has blind spots, and college search tools are no exception. One major limitation is that they can only recommend colleges in their databases for which they have enough data. Smaller, newer, or less "digital" institutions may be under-represented. Schools that serve special populations—such as students returning after military service, or those who plan to start at a community college and transfer—might not rank highly, even if they are excellent fits for particular students.

Another blind spot is that many tools lean heavily on averages and historical patterns. If students like you have typically chosen certain types of colleges in the past, the system assumes you will likely want the same. That can unintentionally reinforce patterns based on race, income, or geography. For example, if a tool has mostly seen high-income suburban students with certain test scores choose expensive private colleges, it may steer similar students in that direction even when those families are more cost-sensitive. If it has learned that students from certain neighborhoods rarely attend schools far from home, it might under-recommend distant options, even for students who are eager to leave.

Finally, some tools include sponsored placements—colleges that pay to appear higher or more often in search results. Even when clearly labeled, these placements can blur the line between neutral recommendation and advertising. Families should not assume that the top result is always the "best" or most appropriate choice. It may simply be the most promoted. Understanding these blind spots doesn't mean abandoning the tools; it means using them with a healthy dose of critical thinking.

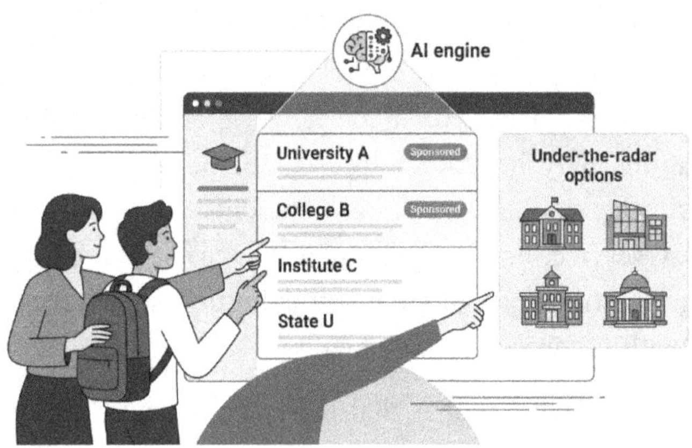

5.5 Student Strategies: Using Tools Without Letting Them Use You

Students don't need to become skeptical of every recommendation, but they do need a strategy. One smart approach is to treat AI-driven search results as "Version 1" of your list, not the final draft. Start by accepting that list as a working set. Then ask yourself: "Which of these schools do I genuinely want to learn more about, and which are here mainly because of my stats?" That simple question shifts you from being a passive recipient of suggestions to an active editor of your own options.

Next, deliberately add "wild cards." Choose at least a few schools that the algorithm didn't surface, based on personal recommendations, trusted adults, or your own research. Maybe a teacher mentions a campus that changed their life, or you learn about a college with a unique program in a niche field you care about. Look those up, even if they don't fit the usual mold. This breaks the echo chamber and gives you a chance to compare the algorithm's comfort zone with your own curiosity.

Finally, use multiple tools. Try two or three different search platforms and notice where they agree and where they differ. If the same college appears high on your list across tools, that's a nudge to look closer. If one tool consistently ignores certain types of schools you care about, that tells you something about its internal assumptions. In all cases, remember that these tools are advisors, not gatekeepers. You are allowed to disagree with them.

Student-Led College Search with AI Support

5.6 Parent Strategies: Guiding Without Overriding

Parents play a crucial role in how these tools are interpreted. It's tempting to use AI-generated "match" labels as hard rules—"You shouldn't even think about this reach school" or "These likely schools are beneath you." Doing so can shut down important conversations about ambition, safety, and risk. Instead, treat the categories as one piece of evidence among many. Ask, "Why do you think this tool put that school in the 'reach' column? What do we know about your strengths that the algorithm might not see?"

You can also help your student balance emotional reactions with practical considerations. When a tool suggests a college, your student has never heard of, instead of dismissing it because "no one talks about it," look together at key data: programs offered, outcomes, cost, and location. Many excellent institutions don't have household-name status. At the same time, if all the tool's suggestions are beyond your family's financial comfort zone, you can gently raise that concern and help your student add more sustainable options.

Another helpful move is to model curiosity about how the tools work. Rather than treating them as mysterious authorities, say things like, “I wonder what information this site uses to make these suggestions. Let’s click on the ‘About’ or ‘Methodology’ section together. Showing your student that it’s normal to question the logic behind a recommendation teaches them a life skill: respect technology, but don’t surrender your judgment to it.

5.7 Using AI as Your Assistant in the Search, Not Your Decider

Just as colleges use AI to organize information about students, you can use AI assistants to organize information about colleges. Once you have a working list, you might ask an AI tool to help you build a comparison table: location, size, key majors, typical class sizes, graduation rates, and broad cost ranges. You can then check those details against official sources. This saves time and gives you a clearer view of how your options stack up on factors that matter to you.

Students can also use AI to turn vague preferences into concrete search criteria. If you know you like "a medium-sized school with a strong sense of community and good support for undecided students," you can ask an AI assistant, "What questions should I ask or what data should I look at to see if a college fits this description?" That way, the AI helps you refine your thinking rather than telling you were to apply. Parents might ask an assistant to outline "Questions to ask a college about mental health services," or "Things to look for in support for first-generation students," and bring those lists into real conversations with admissions teams.

In all of these uses, the assistant is doing what it does best—organizing, suggesting, and clarifying. The decisions about which colleges stay on your list, which to visit, and where to apply remain human decisions, rooted in your family's values, finances, and long-term goals. When you keep that boundary clear, AI becomes a tool that supports your judgment instead of quietly replacing it.

5.8 Checklist for Action: Students

- Use at least two different college search tools. Compare their suggestions, noting where they agree and where they differ, so you see patterns and avoid relying on a single algorithm's view of your options.
- Treat "matches" as a starting point, not a verdict. Take the recommended list and then add at least two schools based on your own research or trusted adults, so your list reflects both data and personal insight.
- Read how each tool makes recommendations. Look for "About" or "Methodology" sections and skim them to understand what information the tool uses and where its blind spots might be.
- Ask an AI assistant to help you compare, not choose.
  Use AI to build simple comparison tables or lists of

questions for colleges, while you keep control over which schools feel right for you.

- Check that your list reflects your real priorities. After using search tools, write down your top three priorities (for example, major strength, distance from home, cost) and see whether your list matches those priorities—or just your stats.

5.9 Checklist for Action: Parents

- Talk with your student about how they're using search tools.
  Ask which sites they like, what those tools are recommending, and how much weight they're giving those suggestions in shaping their list.
- Encourage adding "wild card" schools.
  Suggest that your student include a few colleges based on personal recommendations or independent research, not just AI-generated lists.
- Look beyond name recognition.
  When a recommended college is unfamiliar, help your student look up outcomes, programs, and cost instead of dismissing it because friends haven't heard of it.
- Use AI to generate question lists, not college lists.
  Ask an assistant for questions to bring to counselors or admissions reps about fit, support, and cost, and use those in real conversations.
- Reinforce that tools advise, but don't decide.
  Remind your student that search tools are helpful

filters, not judges of their worth or potential, and that your family's values and circumstances have the final say.

Would you like me to continue with Chapter 6 next, "Essays, Authenticity, and the AI Question," in the same style and structure?

6 Essays, Authenticity, and the AI Question

6.1 "Should I Use AI for My Essay?"

By the time junior year turns into senior year, the entire admissions process can feel like it's circling one big task: the essay. Grades and test scores show what you've done. Activity lists show where you've been. But the essay is supposed to reveal who you are. It's the part that students dread, and admissions officers defend, sometimes in the same breath. In group chats and hallways, one question keeps coming up: "Is it okay to use AI to help with my essay—or is that cheating?"

Students aren't asking this in a vacuum. Many have already used AI tools to help with homework, brainstorm ideas for class projects, or check their grammar. Parents hear conflicting advice from news stories, counselors, and other families. Some say, "everyone is using AI, you'll fall behind if you don't." Others warn, "Colleges can spot AI a mile away; don't risk it." The reality sits in between: AI can be a helpful assistant if you use it wisely and ethically, but it can also erase your voice—and raise serious questions—if you let it take over the steering wheel. Tools don't decide whether an essay is honest. People do.

6.2 How Colleges Are Thinking About AI in Essays

Inside admissions offices, conversations about AI and essays are intense and ongoing. Many colleges now discuss AI use in staff meetings, refine policies year to year, and experiment with tools that flag writing that looks artificially polished or generic. Some institutions have published clear guidelines saying that using AI to generate entire essays is not allowed, but that limited, disclosed use for brainstorming or proofreading may be acceptable. Others are still catching up, leaving students in a gray zone where expectations are unclear, and rumors spread faster than official policies.

What's consistent across many campuses is the value placed on authenticity. Admissions officers read thousands of essays each cycle. Over time, they become very familiar with the rhythms of teenage writing, the kinds of details students include, and the way voice changes between an activities list and a personal narrative. Essays that are heavily AI-generated often feel strangely similar to each other—

smooth but vague, emotionally flat, and full of phrases no teenager actually says. Studies and admissions surveys echo this: AI-written essays tend to sound generic and lack the personal touch readers look for.

At the same time, colleges know that some students will use AI in some way, whether to brainstorm, check grammar, or get feedback. Their main concern is not whether you've ever opened an AI tool. It's whether the essay you submit still represents your thinking, your language, and your story. When officers suspect that a piece was written or heavily rewritten by AI, they don't just question the essay; they start wondering what else in the application might not be fully genuine. That's not a doubt you want to plant.

6.3 Where AI Crosses the Line from Helper to Cheater

Families often ask, "Where exactly is the line?" While each college may define it a little differently, there's a practical way to think about it: if a tool is doing the creative thinking and actual writing for you, you've crossed it. If a tool is helping you think, organize, or polish language that you generated, you're much closer to the ethical side—especially if you're willing to be open about how you used it. Organizations and universities that have begun issuing AI-use guidance often echo the same idea: AI should not write your essay; at most, it should help you make your own writing clearer.

Unethical or risky uses include: asking an AI to "write my essay for me" and submitting that draft with minimal changes; feeding in a prompt and copying a long paragraph directly into your application; or having AI "translate" your ideas into more sophisticated language that no longer sounds like you. These approaches don't just break rules; they make it easier for admissions staff to spot that something is off: the tone doesn't match your short responses; vocabulary jumps oddly; or the story feels generic despite being presented as personal.

More ethical uses—where permitted by a college's policy—tend to start with you, not the tool. You write a rough draft first, then use AI to highlight unclear sentences, spot repetition, or suggest stronger verbs. Or you ask AI for brainstorming questions to help you reflect ("What experiences shaped my interest in engineering?") without letting it produce any actual sentences you'll submit. The content stays yours. The tool helps you see it more clearly. A simple test is this: if an admissions officer asked you to sit in a room and write a version of your essay, could you produce something recognizably similar on your own? If the honest answer is no, the tool has done too much.

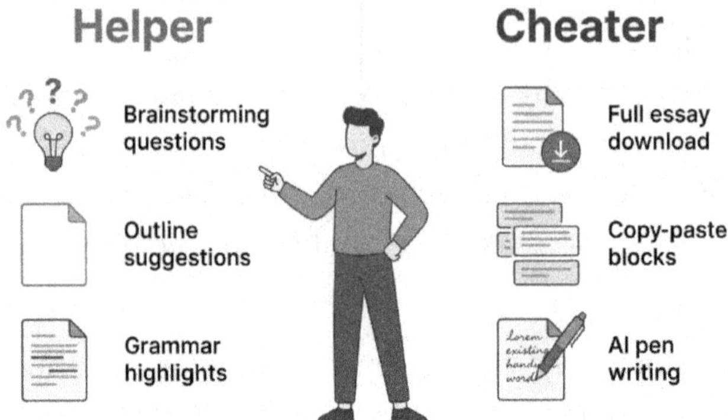

6.4 How Colleges May Detect Heavy AI Use

While no system is perfect, colleges are increasingly combining human judgment with technology to spot essays that lean too heavily on AI. On the human side, readers notice when the main essay's style doesn't match other writing in the application—short answers, activity descriptions, or external writing samples. They also see patterns across many essays in a cycle; if multiple students submit pieces that share unusual phrasing or structure, that raises flags. Readers may not know exactly which tool was used, but they can sense when an essay feels oddly uniform.

On the technology side, some institutions and third-party platforms experiment with AI-detection tools that look for statistical patterns in the text—such as sentence length, predictability, and variation. These tools are far from perfect. They sometimes flag genuine student writing as "AI-like," and they sometimes miss text that humans have edited after being generated. Most colleges that use such tools treat them as early warning systems rather than as automatic verdicts. A flagged essay usually prompts a human review, and in some cases, admissions offices may ask a student for drafts or clarification.

The takeaway is not to live in fear of every typo or well-crafted sentence. It's to understand that if your essay feels to you like something you could never produce on your own, it will likely feel that way to someone else, too. Building your essay around your own draft, your own revisions, and your own voice is the surest way to avoid awkward conversations and to present yourself as a student who's ready for the writing demands of college.

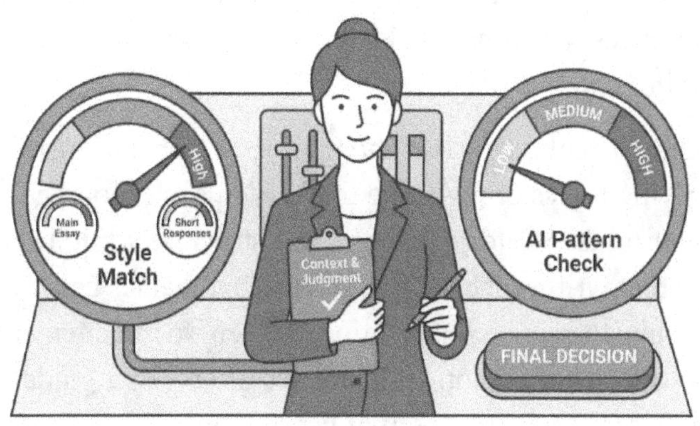

6.5 Using AI as a Brainstorming Coach

Used wisely, AI can be a powerful brainstorming partner at the very beginning of the essay process—before a single sentence is drafted. Many students freeze when asked, "What should I write about?" They assume they need a dramatic story or a perfect narrative arc. Here, AI can help by asking you questions you might not think to ask yourself.

For example, you can prompt an assistant: "Ask me questions to help me remember times when I solved a problem, showed leadership, or changed my perspective. Don't write anything for me; ask questions."

As you answer those questions out loud or in writing, you start to see patterns: recurring themes, values you care about, or moments that genuinely mattered. You might realize that your most important story isn't the big competition you won, but the quieter moment when you are stuck with a difficult class or helped a friend through a tough situation. You can then decide which story feels most like you—and start drafting in your own words. At this stage, AI is more like a mirror than a ghostwriter. It reflects your experiences to you in clearer angles without inventing anything new.

For parents, this is a moment to step back. Instead of supplying topics or rewriting drafts, you can encourage your student to use AI for questions and structure while keeping the actual writing theirs. Ask them what themes came up in the brainstorming conversation. Listen for excitement or hesitation. Those emotional cues are often better guides to a strong essay than any external list of "top topics."

6.6 Polishing Without Losing Your Voice

Once you have a draft, it's natural to want help making it clearer and tighter. This is where tools that check grammar, suggest clearer wording, or flag repetitive phrases can be genuinely useful—as long as you stay in control. You might ask an AI assistant, "Show me sentences that are confusing or wordy," or "Point out where I repeat myself." Then you decide how to revise. The goal is to sound like your best self on a good writing day, not like a completely different person.

One useful strategy is to revise in layers. First, read your essay out loud. Mark any place where you stumble or feel that the wording doesn't sound like something you'd say. Fix those spots yourself. Then, if you choose, run the draft through an AI tool to catch technical issues—missing words, unclear pronoun references, or inconsistent verb tenses. When the tool suggests changes, ask yourself with each one: "Does this still sound like me?" If a suggestion makes your sentence smoother but changes your tone, trust your ear over the machine.

Parents can help here by reading for voice, not perfection. Instead of line-editing every sentence, ask, “Does this sound like you when you’re telling a story?” If not, encourage your student to rewrite in their own way. Essays that are a bit rough around the edges but deeply personal often stay with readers longer than flawless but generic ones.

6.7 Student Story: Malik and the Over-Polished Draft

Malik, a strong student with big responsibilities at home, struggled to find time for his essay. After weeks of procrastination, he panicked and pasted his main prompt into an AI tool, asking it to write a draft based on a few short notes about his life. The result looked impressive: smooth sentences, thoughtful reflections, and a neat ending that tied everything together. Grateful and exhausted, he made only small edits and shared it with his English teacher for feedback.

His teacher’s first reaction wasn’t praise; it was concern. “This doesn’t sound like you,” she said gently. The voice in the essay didn't match the writing Malik had done in class. The vocabulary was oddly formal. The story, while technically about his experiences, felt like it belonged to a polished narrator, not the quick-witted, direct student she knew. She asked Malik to talk through the story out loud. As he spoke, different details emerged—messier, funnier, more specific. That conversation led him to start over, drafting by hand this time, with the AI document closed. The new essay looked less perfect on the surface, but it sounded like Malik.

What changed wasn't just the text. It was Malik's sense of ownership. In the first version, he couldn't have explained why each sentence was there; they were mostly the tool's choices. In the second, he could trace every idea back to something he had lived or thought. That confidence made it easier to talk about his essay in interviews and to feel proud of what he submitted. His experience shows the difference between using AI to avoid work and using support (from teachers, friends, and light tools) to do the work in an honest way.

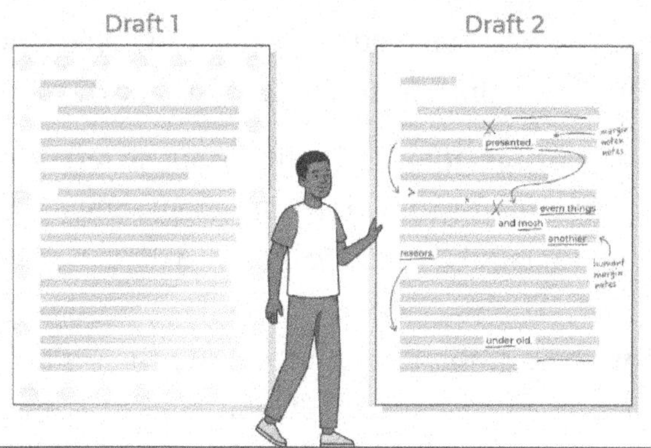

6.8 Parent Story: Mrs. Chen and the "Too Perfect" Essay

Mrs. Chen watched her daughter, Lila, stress over essay drafts for weeks. Wanting to help, she suggested trying an AI tool "just to get some ideas." Lila fed in a rough paragraph, and within seconds the tool returned a crisp, organized essay. Lila was relieved, but Mrs. Chen felt uneasy. The essay didn't sound like the sometimes-sarcastic, detail-loving teenager she knew. It sounded like an adult giving a polished speech. Still, with deadlines looming, it was tempting to accept the draft and move on.

After a restless night, Mrs. Chen decided to be honest. She told Lila, "I'm proud of how hard you've worked, and I understand why you tried this. But if an admissions officer asked you to rewrite this by hand tomorrow, could you? Would it come out anything like this?" Lila hesitated and admitted it wouldn't. Together, they agreed to use the AI draft differently: as a mirror to see what structure and themes were working, not as the final product. Lila pulled out three ideas from the AI-generated essay that truly belonged to her, then wrote a new draft from scratch in her own words.

This approach took more time, but it left Mrs. Chen more comfortable and Lila more confident. They also decided, as a family rule, that they would be willing to explain any AI use a college asked. That simple test—"Would we be comfortable telling an admissions officer how we used this tool?"—became their guide for what was acceptable and what crossed a line.

6.9 Family Guardrails for Essay-Related AI Use

Because colleges' policies differ and technology keeps evolving, it helps to set your own family guardrails around AI and essays. One helpful rule is: "AI can help us think and polish, but not create or translate our voice." That means you allow brainstorming, question suggestions, and grammar checks. Still, you avoid wholesale drafting, heavy rephrasing that changes tone, or translating an essay written in another language in a way that misrepresents writing skills. If you're not sure whether something is okay, ask, "Would we be comfortable describing this use honestly in an interview or email to admissions?" If the answer is no, don't do it.

You can also agree on process guardrails. For example, the student writes a first draft without AI, then shares it with a trusted adult (teacher, counselor, or parent) before using any tools. Only after human feedback does the student use light AI assistance for clarity or proofreading, if at all. Throughout, the student keeps versions, showing how the essay evolved. That not only protects integrity but also provides a record in case a college ever questions authorship. The goal is not to be paranoid; it's to be prepared and principled.

These guardrails also teach a bigger lesson: in a world where shortcuts are easy, and tools are powerful, your reputation for honesty and your ability to express yourself are long-term assets. The essay is one of the first high-stakes places where students practice protecting those assets. With clear family guidelines, AI becomes a tool that supports growth instead of tempting you into decisions you might later regret.

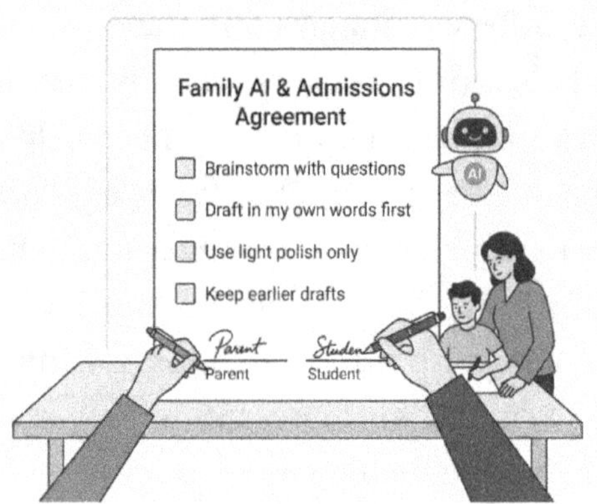

6.10 Checklist for Action: Students

- Write a "zero-tech" mini-draft first.
  Spend 20–30 minutes handwriting a rough response to a prompt before opening any AI tool, so your starting point is fully your own.
- Use AI only for questions and clarity, not content.
  Ask assistants to generate questions or point out

confusing sections but avoid copying any sentences they write into your final essay.

- Read your essay out loud to someone who knows you.
  Ask if it sounds like your humor, your phrasing, your way of telling stories—and revise anything that feels off.
- Keep every draft and major revision.
  Save versions as you go so you can show a clear writing process if anyone ever asks how your essay developed.
- Apply the "hand-write" test.
  Ask yourself if you could recreate a similar essay by hand in a proctored room; if not, scale back your reliance on tools and rebuild in your own voice.

6.11 Checklist for Action: Parents

- Ask your student how they're thinking about AI and essays.
  Start an open conversation about their temptations, fears, and questions before you suggest any tools or rules.
- Set a shared line you won't cross.
  Agree that AI will not be used to write full drafts or fundamentally rewrite your student's voice, and put that commitment in writing if it helps.
- Focus your feedback on authenticity, not perfection.
  When reading drafts, prioritize whether the essay

reveals who your student is rather than whether every sentence is flawless.

- Encourage human feedback before tool feedback. Help your student connect with teachers or counselors for early input, so they don't lean on AI as their first or only critic.
- Be ready to explain your family's approach if asked.
  Talk through how you'd describe your AI use in an email or meeting with admissions; if you'd feel uneasy sharing the full story, reconsider your approach.

7 AI in Scholarship Matching and Financial Aid

7.1 The Late-Night Scholarship Search That Never Ends

Picture a student sitting at the kitchen table with a laptop open, long after everyone else has gone to bed. The college list is mostly set. Applications are underway. Now the focus has shifted to an even more stressful question: "How are we going to pay for this?" The student types "scholarships for seniors" into a search bar and is flooded with results—national awards, local grants, niche programs. After an hour of scrolling, everything blurs together. The student gives up for the night, feeling like they're missing chances but not sure where to start.

This scene is so common that it has a name among recruiters: the scholarship spiral. Families know help is out there, but the search process is confusing and exhausting. That's where a new wave of AI-powered scholarship tools has stepped in. These platforms promise to "match" students with relevant scholarships, remind them of deadlines, and sometimes even pre-fill parts of applications. Used wisely, they can save hours and surface opportunities your student would never find on their own. Used blindly, they can create a false sense of security and leave money on the table.

Manual Search

Matched & Organized

7.2 How AI-Powered Scholarship Matching Actually Works

Most AI-driven scholarship platforms follow a similar pattern. First, they ask the student to create a profile with basic demographics, GPA range, potential major, extracurricular activities, and sometimes more personal details such as family background, work experience, or future goals. Some tools also import information from resumes or previous applications. All of this becomes structured data that the system can analyze at scale.

Next, the AI compares that profile to a large database of scholarships. Instead of you reading every eligibility list by hand, the system scans requirements, major, location, GPA thresholds, special interests, demographic criteria—and calculates how well each one fits your profile. It scores and ranks scholarships, often tagging some as “Top Matches,” others as “Good Fits,” and some as “Low Priority.” Advanced systems continue to learn from what you click, save, or ignore, refining recommendations over time so they become more tailored.

Finally, many of these tools add automation around the edges. They send reminders as deadlines approach, suggest ways to reuse essay content across multiple applications, and sometimes autofill basic information into forms when integrations are available. In the best cases, they function like a personal scholarship assistant—sorting noise, surfacing real possibilities, and helping keep you on track with timelines you might otherwise miss.

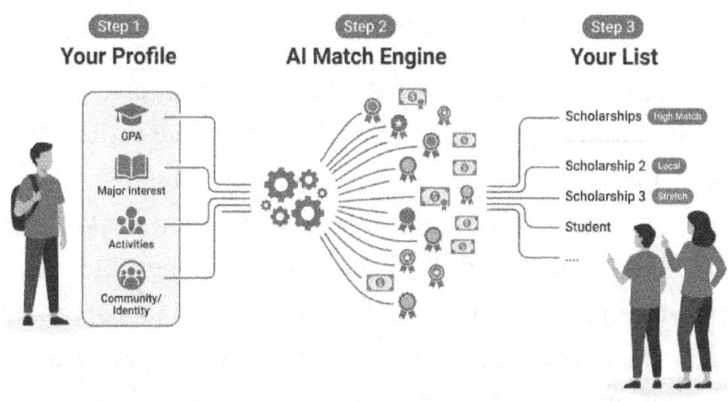

7.3 The Promise: Finding Money You'd Never See Otherwise

The biggest upside of AI-powered scholarship tools is reach. Instead of relying on whatever your school posts on a bulletin board or what you happen to find in a generic search, these platforms can scan thousands of opportunities, including small or niche awards you might otherwise miss. Some focus on particular career paths, some on communities or service, and some on very specific combinations of interests—things most students wouldn't think to search for directly.

These tools can also personalize recommendations to reduce wasted effort. If you're a first-generation student interested in nursing who works part-time and volunteers in your community, the AI can prioritize scholarships that value exactly those traits instead of just sending you every award tagged "healthcare." Over time, as you mark which scholarships you plan to apply for and which you skip, the system learns your preferences and becomes more precise. That means more time spent on realistic, aligned opportunities and less on long-shots or irrelevant ones.

For busy families, that efficiency matters. Students juggling school, jobs, and activities don't have endless hours to dig through database after database. Parents may want to help, but they can only search so much after work. AI can act like a smart filter, bringing a manageable set of opportunities into view so the family can focus on what really matters: deciding which ones are worth the effort and crafting strong applications.

BEFORE

AFTER

7.4 Where AI-Driven Scholarship Tools Can Fall Short

Despite their promise, AI scholarship platforms are not magic, and they have clear limitations. One is coverage. No tool has every piece of scholarship in existence. Some databases lean heavily on national awards and miss local or school-specific opportunities. Others are built around particular donor networks or regions. If you rely only on one platform, you may never see smaller community-based scholarships that have fewer applicants and higher odds of success.

Another limitation is accuracy. AI can match based on obvious criteria—major, GPA, location—but it cannot read the nuances of every scholarship's intent. It might suggest awards that look like a fit on paper but require commitments or qualifications you don't actually meet, such as majoring in a specific field all four years or attending a certain kind of institution. It may also miss qualitative elements, such as fit with a particular mission or a preference for hands-on service over academic research. That's why reading the fine print yourself still matters.

There's also the issue of overload in a new form. Some tools generate long lists of "matches" that look impressive but are unrealistic based on your time, energy, or the number of essays required. If you treat every recommendation as equally urgent, you can burn out quickly. AI can suggest opportunities, but it cannot know that you also have a heavy sports season, a family job, or other responsibilities. Without human judgment, a "smart" list can still become another source of stress.

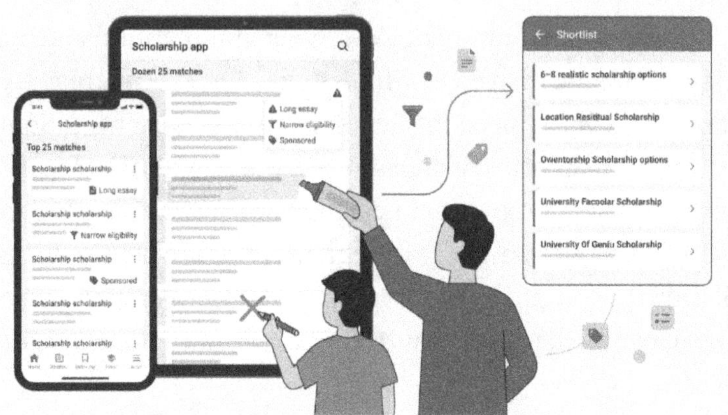

7.5 How Colleges Use AI in Their Own Financial Aid Strategies

AI isn't only on the student side of the money conversation; colleges themselves use predictive analytics and AI-informed models to guide how they offer aid. Financial aid offices and enrollment teams analyze patterns from past years: how different levels and types of aid influenced whether students enrolled, stayed for multiple years, or transferred out. With that history, they build models to estimate what kind of scholarship or grant package might be needed to encourage a student with a certain profile actually to attend.

These models don't change your family's financial needs, but they do influence how schools distribute limited funds. For example, if data shows that offering a slightly larger grant to students from a specific region significantly increases enrollment, a college might direct more aid there.

Some use AI to identify students who are "on the edge" financially and at risk of not enrolling or returning, so they can target extra support where it will prevent melt-out or dropout. Done thoughtfully, this can improve access and retention; done poorly, it can tilt resources toward students who look more "profitable" on paper rather than those with the greatest need.

From your family's perspective, this means two things. First, financial aid offers are not just about you; they are shaped by institutional strategy and prediction. Second, reaching out to financial aid offices to explain your situation, ask about additional options, or clarify special circumstances still matters. AI can suggest what the average student "like you" might do, but a real conversation can highlight factors the model doesn't see—family illness, job loss, or unique obligations—that should influence your package.

Financial Aid Strategy Family Decision

7.6 Student Strategies: Using AI to Hunt for Scholarships Without Getting Lost

For students, the temptation with AI-driven tools is either to ignore them completely or to treat them as all-knowing. A middle path works best. Start by creating a thoughtful profile on one or two reputable platforms. Take your time entering details about activities, work, and goals, since those often unlock more specific matches. Then, when you see your initial list, resist the urge to "apply to everything." Instead, sort opportunities into three buckets: high priority (strong fit, realistic requirements), medium (interesting but more competitive or time-consuming), and low (long shots or less aligned)

Next, set a realistic application goal. For example, you might commit to applying to all high-priority scholarships and to two or three from the medium group. Use the AI tool's reminders to keep track of deadlines, but also put them on your own calendar or planner. For each scholarship, check eligibility yourself—don't assume the match is perfect. Skim the criteria, note any extra requirements (like recommendation letters or special essays), and estimate how much time each one will take. This helps you avoid last-minute rushes where quality suffers.

Finally, use AI assistants on your side in a way that mirrors your approach to essays: as helpers, not authors. Let them generate checklists for each scholarship, suggest ways to organize similar prompts, or help you build a schedule. But keep the core of your applications—your stories, your reasons, your tone—your own. Scholarship committees, like admissions teams, are drawn to specificity and authenticity, not polished sameness.

[Diagram 6 description, blue-and-white palette, icons + humans: A student's screen showing a scholarship dashboard split into three columns: "High Priority," "Medium," "Low." Each tile shows the deadline and the effort level. Next to the screen is a paper planner where the student writes specific application dates. A small AI assistant icon provides a checklist, while the student checks off tasks.]

7.7 Parent Strategies: Supporting Search Without Taking Over

Parents often experience the financial side of admissions with a different kind of stress. You may feel a strong urge to "fix it" by taking over the scholarship search, filling out forms, or pushing your student to apply to every possible award. AI-powered tools can either amplify that pressure or help you channel it productively. One helpful approach is to take on the role of organizer and coach, rather than primary applicant. You might help vet which platforms to use, read privacy policies, or identify local scholarships from community organizations, while your student completes the personal parts of applications.

You can also use AI tools yourself to make sense of the big picture. For example, you might ask an AI assistant to help you compare the estimated costs of several colleges side by side, including projected aid, and then bring that summary into a financial aid meeting. Or you might ask for a list of questions to ask scholarship providers or financial aid officers about renewal conditions, hidden fees, or work-study expectations. This keeps you engaged on the strategic level without blurring the line between your voice and your student's voice in applications.

At the same time, be mindful of your student's bandwidth. Work with them to set a reasonable scholarship application target—enough to matter, not so many that it burns them out. Encourage them to schedule scholarship work in smaller, regular blocks instead of last-minute marathons. Recognize that saying "no" to some opportunities is not laziness; it's making room to do a better job on the ones that fit best.

7.8 Guardrails: Keeping Data, Time, and Expectations in Check

Because scholarships and financial-aid tools often ask for sensitive information, families should set clear guardrails before diving in. Start with data. Agree on what you will and will not share on third-party sites: academic information and basic demographics may be fine, but social security numbers, banking details, or highly personal stories should stay within official application portals or trusted institutions. Review privacy policies together and look for clear explanations of how data is used, stored, and shared. If a platform feels vague or overly intrusive, you can choose not to use it.

Next, set time and expectation guardrails. Decide how many hours per week your student can realistically devote to scholarships during peak seasons, and stick to that limit. If an AI tool keeps suggesting more opportunities, remember that the goal is not to apply to everything; it is to apply well to the right things. You can also set an emotional guardrail: agree that your family's sense of worth or success is not tied to the number of scholarships won. Financial support is important, but it is not a measure of character or potential.

With these guardrails in place, AI becomes a way to extend your reach, not a way to outsource your judgment. You decide which tools to trust, which opportunities to chase, and how to balance hope with realism. In a landscape where money and emotion are tightly linked, that shared clarity can prevent misunderstandings and keep your family working together instead of pulling in different directions.

[Diagram 8 description, blue-and-white palette, icons + humans: A "Scholarship Guardrails" road graphic. Along the road labeled "Funding Journey" are guardrails labeled "Data Safety," "Time Limits," and "Realistic Expectations." AI scholarship icons travel on the road, but the guardrails keep them from veering into unsafe zones. A family walks alongside, referring to a simple written guideline sheet.]

7.9 Checklist for Action: Students

- Build one strong profile, then refine it.
  Choose a reputable scholarship platform, create a detailed profile, and update it as your activities or plans change so matches stay accurate.

- Sort your matches into priority levels.
  Divide recommended scholarships into high, medium, and low priority based on fit, effort required, and deadlines, instead of trying to treat them all the same.

- Put deadlines in your own system.
  Copy key scholarship dates from the platform into a calendar or planner you actually use, so you're not relying solely on app notifications.

- Use AI to organize, not to write your applications.
  Let an assistant help create checklists or schedules, but keep essays, answers, and interview prep in your own words and style.

- Combine AI tools with local research.
  Ask your counselor, community groups, and workplaces about scholarships and then add those to your list, so you don't miss opportunities the algorithms overlook.

7.10 Checklist for Action: Parents

- Set shared rules for data and tools.
  Decide together which scholarship and finance tools you trust, what information you'll share, and which platforms you'll avoid.

- Help identify local and niche scholarships.
  Use your networks—employers, community organizations, faith groups, unions—to find awards that may not appear in big AI databases.
- Support a realistic application plan.
  Work with your student to set a weekly time budget and target number of applications, balancing scholarship work with school, rest, and family life.
- Use AI to prepare for financial conversations.
  Ask an assistant to help you outline questions and gather cost comparisons before meeting with financial aid offices, then verify details directly with the college.
- Keep the focus on options, not pressure.
  Remind your student that scholarships are important, but they're one piece of a larger financial and educational plan—not a measure of their worth or your family's value.

8 The New Metrics: Predictive Yield and Enrollment Algorithms

8.1 Why Parents Need to Understand "Yield" Now

Most parents grew up thinking of college admissions in simple terms: your student applies, the college decides, and then you choose from whatever offers come in. Behind the scenes, though, colleges are asking a different question long before you ever see an acceptance letter: "If we admit this student, how likely are they to say yes?" That likelihood has a name—yield—, and it's increasingly shaped by AI and predictive analytics rather than just gut instinct.

Yield used to be something colleges measured after the fact. They looked at how many admitted students actually enrolled and adjusted strategies for the next year. Now, AI tools allow them to estimate yield for each prospect while decisions are being made. Those estimates can influence everything from how much merit aid is offered to how many students a school admits in the first round. For families, that means your student is not just being evaluated on "can they do the work?" but also on "will they actually come?" Understanding that shift helps you interpret admissions and financial-aid outcomes with clearer eyes.

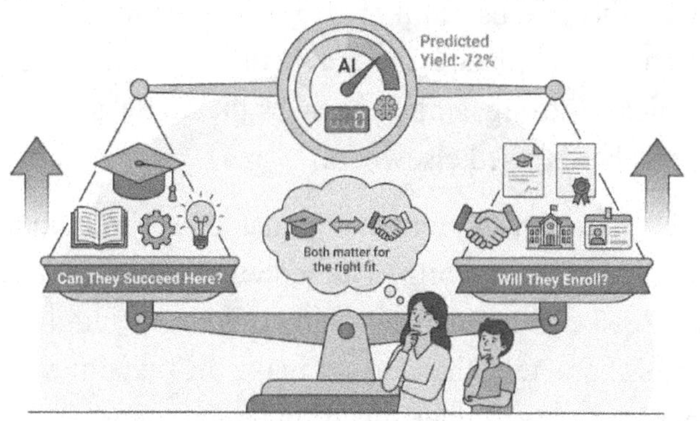

Balancing Success and Enrollment Factors

8.2 What Predictive Yield Models Actually Do

Predictive yield models start with data—lots of it. Colleges feed in information about past applicants and enrollees: academic profiles, geography, application timing, visit history, financial aid packages, and engagement patterns (emails opened, events attended, forms completed). The model learns which combinations of factors tend to produce a "yes" versus a "no." Once trained, it can look at a current applicant and estimate the probability that they will enroll if admitted and offered a particular aid package.

These models don't replace traditional evaluation. Admissions officers still decide whether a student is a good academic and personal fit. But once a student clears that bar, yield predictions may influence where they fall in the admit/waitlist/deny balance or how aggressively the college courts them. A student who looks very likely to enroll may receive more personalized outreach and an aid package tuned to "just enough" to secure their commitment. A student who seems unlikely to say yes might get less attention or be placed on the waitlist, even if they are academically strong, simply because the model suggests that the slot is better used elsewhere.

It's important to remember that these predictions are about behavior, not worth. The model is trying to minimize empty seats and financial surprises, not judging your student's character. That doesn't make the outcomes feel any less personal, but it does mean that sometimes a near-miss or unexpected denial has more to do with an institution's forecast than with your student's potential.

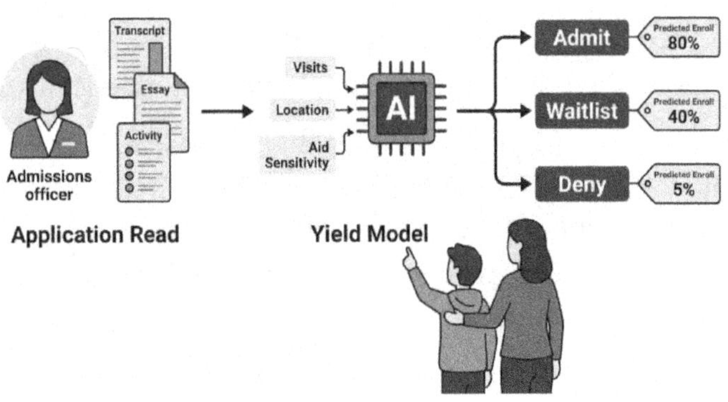

8.3 How These Models Change Admissions Strategy

When a college has a reasonably accurate yield model, it stops thinking about admissions purely in terms of "How many students can we admit?". It starts thinking in terms of "How many students with which probabilities do we need to admit to land at our target class size?" That's why you sometimes hear about "over-enrolled" or "under-enrolled" classes—years when the model's guesses were off. When models are accurate, however, colleges can admit fewer students overall while still filling the class, which in turn can drive down published admit rates and make the school look more selective.

These models also shape how colleges spread their offers across different groups. If a school's data suggests that in-state students with certain profiles almost always enroll when admitted, it may be more cautious about extending large merit offers to them, focusing aid instead on students who are more uncertain or who have many competing offers. Conversely, if out-of-state students historically require stronger financial packages to enroll, the model may flag them as needing more aid or more personalized outreach. In plain terms: the same academic profile might lead to different treatment depending on how the college believes you'll behave.

For parents, it's helpful to see admissions decisions not just as yes/no judgments but as the output of a complicated balancing act. Colleges are trying to hit enrollment, budget, and diversity targets all at once. Predictive yield models are tools they use in that juggling act. That doesn't make the process fair in every case—but it does explain why two very similar students can receive different outcomes or offers from the same school.

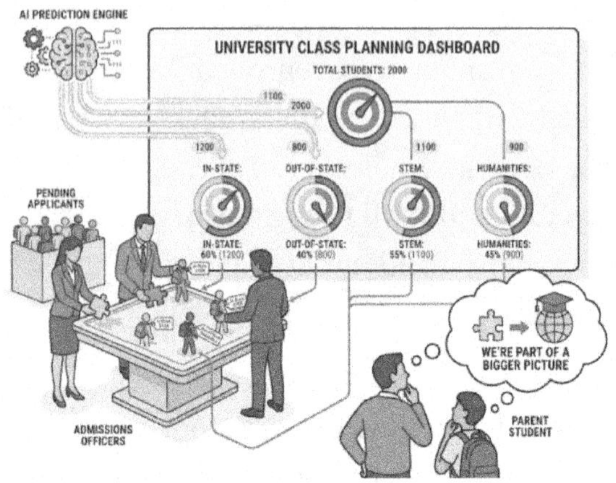

8.4 Why Demonstrated Interest Matters More Than It Used To

Demonstrated interest—the ways a student shows they're truly considering a school—has always mattered a little. In an AI-shaped world, it often matters more, especially at schools that track it closely. Every campus visit, webinar attendance, email open, portal login, or conversation with a rep becomes a data point in the yield model's understanding of how serious your student is. From the model's perspective, a student who has repeatedly engaged looks more likely to enroll than someone who applied without much prior contact.

This doesn't mean you need to treat the college as a full-time job. It does mean that when a school is genuinely high on your student's list, it's wise to act like it. That can include: making sure emails don't go to spam, attending at least one virtual or in-person event, asking thoughtful questions, and using the application to articulate specific reasons the school fits. For parents, encouraging a modest but real level of engagement—rather than either apathy or overkill—helps ensure the model doesn't misread your student as indifferent.

It's also important to know that some colleges, especially highly selective ones, openly say they don't consider demonstrated interest. Others quietly factor it in. The more transparent schools are about this, the easier it is to plan. When in doubt, a reasonable level of genuine engagement is rarely wasted: even if the data isn't fed directly into a model, it can inform how human readers perceive the seriousness of your application.

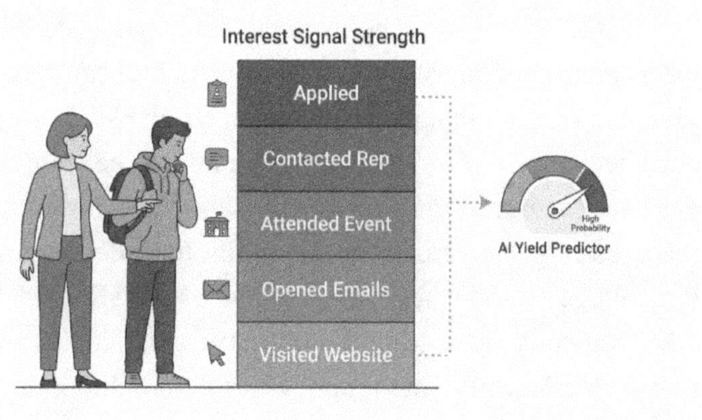

8.5 Parent-Focused Financial Scenarios in a Predictive World

To make this concrete, let's walk through three families facing the same college but different predictive scenarios. These aren't exact replicas of any one family, but they combine patterns that admissions and financial-aid teams talk about all the time.

Scenario A: The "Highly Likely" In-State Student

- Your student is in-state for a public university.
- Their academics fit well with the school's typical admitted profile.
- They've visited campus, engaged with emails, and attended a virtual event.
- The college's model predicts a high chance of enrollment if admitted, even with a moderate aid offer.

In this case, the school might admit your student and offer a standard merit package—not the highest they could give, but enough that past students in similar situations have accepted. From your side, the offer might feel fair but not generous, especially if you know families whose students received larger awards. The key point to understand is that the college's model sees your student as a "safe bet," which can, ironically, lead to less aggressive aid. This is where a polite, well-documented appeal can sometimes make a difference.

Scenario B: The "Cross-Shopping" Out-of-State Student

- Your student is out-of-state and considering several competing colleges.
- Their academics are strong, and their profile fits well with the school's strategic goals.

- Engagement has been steady but not intense; the college senses they have options.
- The model predicts your student will enroll only if the aid package is competitive.

Here, the school might offer a more generous merit- or need-based package, not purely out of generosity, but because the model suggests they'll lose your student otherwise. Your family's seriousness, the strength of your student's profile, and the college's need for out-of-state enrollment all combine to push the offer higher. From your perspective, you may feel pleasantly surprised. It's still important to compare long-term affordability across schools, because sometimes a higher "discount" still leads to a higher out-of-pocket cost than a lower-priced option.

Scenario C: The "Uncertain Fit" With High Need

- Your student is a strong fit academically but comes from a family with significant financial need.
- Engagement has been mixed—some contact, but fewer visits or events due to work, distance, or cost.
- The college's model predicts a real risk that, without a substantial aid offer, your student won't enroll or might struggle to persist.

In a thoughtful system, this is exactly the kind of student a college might flag for extra support: additional grant aid, targeted outreach, or special programs designed to close gaps. In a less thoughtful system, the model may suggest that the cost of meeting your need outweighs the likelihood you'll enroll, leading to a modest package that makes attendance unrealistic. From your side of the table, this can feel like the college "doesn't want you enough," when in fact it reflects institutional limits and a cold calculation that doesn't fully capture your student's determination or potential.

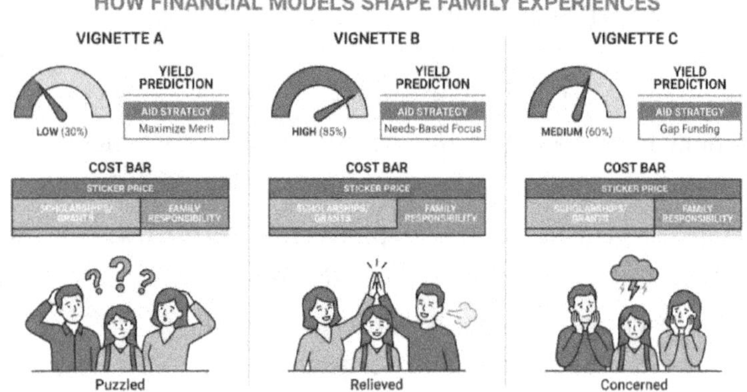

8.6 How AI Is Changing Financial Aid Conversations for Parents

Beyond admissions, AI is also reshaping how families get information about cost and aid. Many colleges now use bots or virtual assistants to answer routine questions about forms, deadlines, and basic terminology. Some tools can walk you through an award letter step by step, explaining the difference between grants, loans, and work-study in plain language. Others allow you to upload award offers from multiple colleges and see a simplified comparison of real out-of-pocket costs. These tools are designed to help parents who don't speak "financial-aid" as a second language.

From a parent's perspective, this can be a huge relief. Instead of waiting on hold to ask, "What does this line mean?" you can get quick, clear explanations at any time of day. However, AI assistants can't see your full financial picture, your retirement plans, or your tolerance for debt. They also can't weigh emotional factors like closeness to home or your student's mental health needs. That's why AI should be a first pass—a way to get oriented—before you have deeper conversations with human financial-aid counselors, financial planners, or trusted advisors.

You can also use general AI assistants to prepare for those human conversations. For example, you might ask, "What questions should I ask a financial-aid officer when comparing award letters?" or "What information should I gather before calling about a special-circumstances appeal?" The tool can help you build a checklist, but you still decide which questions matter most to your family's situation.

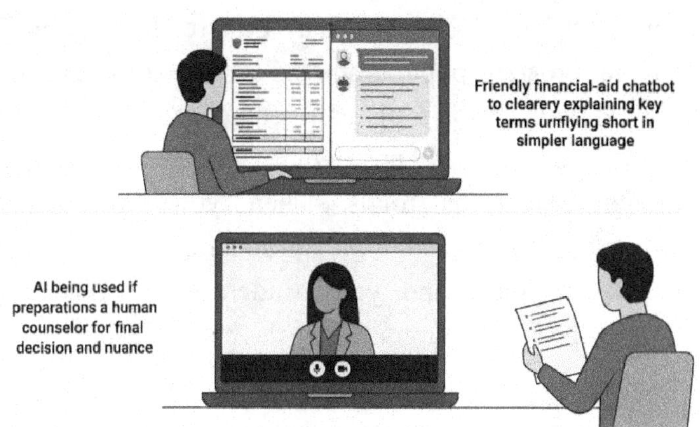

8.7 Deeper Financial Scenarios: Putting It All Together

To see how these pieces—yield, aid strategy, and AI tools—intertwine, consider three more detailed, parent-focused scenarios.

Scenario 1: Two Acceptances, Very Different Bills Your student is admitted to College X and College Y.

- College X has a high sticker price but offers a large merit scholarship.
- College Y has a lower sticker price and a modest grant.
- After aid, the annual out-of-pocket cost is surprisingly similar.

Behind the scenes, College X's predictive model may be using high merit offers to compete for students with specific profiles. College Y may be stretching limited aid across a broader population. As a parent, you can use AI-based comparison tools or a general assistant to create a side-by-side table: total cost, grants/scholarships, loans, and estimated four-year totals. Then you can factor in non-numeric considerations: graduation rates, support services, distance, and your student's fit. The "bigger scholarship" is not automatically the better deal.

Scenario 2: The Gap Between Aid and Reality Your student receives an award letter that technically covers "need" but leaves a gap you know will be hard to bridge.

- The package includes a mix of grants, loans, and work-study.
- The college's model may assume families will stretch to cover the remaining amount.

Here, AI can help you prepare an appeal. You might use a tool to help draft a clear, respectful letter that explains changed circumstances (job loss, medical bills, elder care), lists your current obligations, and asks whether any additional grant aid or payment options are available. The letter should come from you or your student in your own words, with AI only helping with structure or clarity—not writing the story. Then you bring documentation and questions to a human financial-aid officer, who has the authority to override the model when the numbers don't tell the whole truth.

Scenario 3: Balancing Debt and Dreams
Your student falls in love with a college that, even after aid, will require significant loans. Another school is more affordable but less exciting.

- Yield models and aid strategies have done their job for the expensive college; the offer is enough to make the dream feel "just barely" possible.
- You're torn between wanting to support that dream and worrying about long-term debt.

In this situation, you can use AI as a calculator and explainer. Ask it to show what monthly payments might look like at different loan amounts, how those payments compare to entry-level salaries in your student's intended field, and how loan scenarios could affect goals like graduate school or homeownership. Again, you verify specifics with real lenders and financial aid staff, but the AI helps you visualize trade-offs. Then, as a family, you talk honestly about values: Is this level of debt aligned with your comfort? Are there ways to start at a more affordable school and transfer? The model predicted what might entice you. You decide whether that enticement is wise.

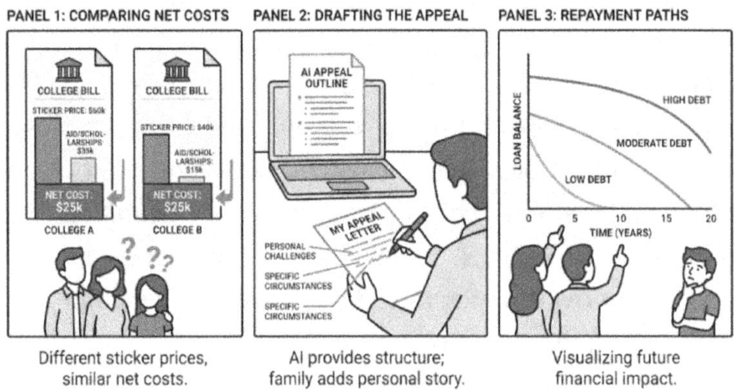

Different sticker prices, similar net costs.
AI provides structure; family adds personal story.
Visualizing future financial impact.

8.8 Guardrails for Parents: Questions to Ask and Lines to Hold

In a world where algorithms influence who gets admitted and how aid is distributed, parents need their own guardrails. One guardrail is curiosity. Get comfortable asking colleges questions like:

- “Do you consider demonstrated interest or predictive models when shaping your class?”
- “How do you ensure financial-aid decisions are fair to students with high need?”

- "If our situation changes, what is the process for review?"

Another guardrail is transparency within your family. Be clear with your student early about what your family can realistically afford without risking retirement or essential stability. That doesn't mean shutting down dreams; it means setting a framework so that when offers arrive, you have a shared baseline for what counts as "manageable." Predictive models are built on the behavior of past families. You don't have to replay their script if it doesn't fit your circumstances.

Finally, hold a line on honesty and agency. Use AI tools to understand jargon, compare offers, and plan questions—but keep all major decisions rooted in human conversation and shared values. If you ever feel pressured into a choice because "the system says this is what families like us do," take a step back. Your story is not a data point. Models can inform; they shouldn't rule.

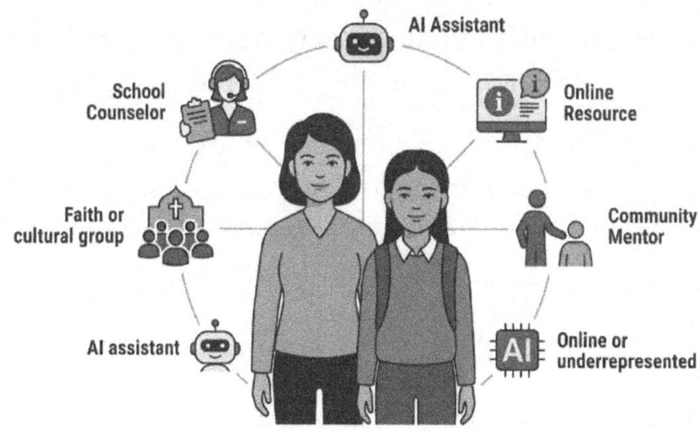

8.9 Checklist for Action: Students

- Show genuine interest where it's real.
  For colleges you truly like, take a few specific steps—open emails, attend an event, ask questions—so your interest is visible without becoming overwhelming.

- Ask how each college uses interest and data.
  When talking to admissions reps, listen for whether they track engagement and how they describe using it, so you're not guessing about what matters.

- Keep your options open across cost levels.
  Build a list that includes schools you love at different price points, so you're not trapped if yield-driven aid strategies make some offers unaffordable.

- Use AI to clarify, not decide.
  Let assistants help you understand award letters and loan terms, but bring questions and concerns back to your family and counselors for real decisions.

- Remember you're more than a prediction.
  Treat models and metrics as background noise, not a verdict on your worth or future; your choices and efforts still shape what happens next.

8.10 Checklist for Action: Parents

- Learn the basics of yield and predictive models.
  Familiarize yourself with concepts such as "yield," "demonstrated interest," and "enrollment targets" so that admissions and aid patterns make more sense.

- Talk openly about the budget before offers arrive.
  Share a realistic range of what your family can contribute each year, so aid packages are evaluated against a clear, shared understanding.
- Use AI assistants to prep, then talk to humans.
  Ask tools to help you decode jargon and frame questions, but rely on conversations with financial-aid officers for final clarity and decisions.
- Compare total four-year costs, not just first-year aid.
  Look at renewal requirements, likely increases, and long-term loan implications, not just the first year's "sticker vs discount" comparison.
- Model calm, values-based decision-making.
  Show your student that you'll use all the tools available—but that in the end, family priorities, financial health, and their well-being matter more than any algorithm's prediction.

9 Equity, Bias, and Fairness in AI-Driven Recruitment

9.1 Why This Chapter Is Different

If you or your student come from a community that has not always been treated fairly in education—Black, Latinx, Indigenous, first-generation, rural, immigrant, low-income, undocumented, students with disabilities—you already know that "systems" can feel like obstacles as much as supports. AI-driven recruitment is one more system layered on top. It can either quietly widen the gap or help close it, depending on how colleges build and use it, and on how your family responds.

This chapter speaks directly to that reality. It explains how algorithms can overlook or misread underrepresented students, how they *can* be used to expand opportunity, and how you—as a student or parent—can act strategically without trying to carry the whole system on your back. We'll keep coming back to one core idea: your story is more than your data, but you need to know how your data is being read so your story doesn't get lost.

9.2 How Algorithms Can Miss Underrepresented Students

AI systems learn from patterns in past data. That sounds neutral, but past data in education is anything *but* neutral. It reflects decades of unequal school funding, uneven access to advanced courses, differences in counseling support, and biases in standardized testing. When an algorithm trains on that history without adjustment, it often carries those inequalities forward.

Here are some common ways that happen:

- Engagement is misread as interest.
  Models may treat campus visits, multiple event attendances, and frequent portal logins as strong signals of interest. Students who work after school, care for siblings, can't travel, or share devices with family have fewer chances to generate those

signals—even when they care deeply about the school.

- Resource gaps look like readiness gaps.
  Algorithms that rely heavily on AP/IB courses, test scores, or school "track records" can under-estimate students from underfunded schools. If your school didn't *offer* advanced coursework, the model may see you as less prepared when, in reality, you did the most with what you had.
- "At risk" labels reflect missing context.
  On the retention side, models sometimes flag underrepresented students as "at risk" of dropping out at higher rates. That flag might trigger helpful support—or it might feed stereotypes about who "belongs" in rigorous programs. The label is based on limited data, not on the full story of a student's determination or support network.

None of this means AI is always working against underrepresented students. It does mean families should assume that models need context to read their student accurately—and that providing that context is an act of self-advocacy, not complaining.

9.3 Underrepresented Students and the "Engagement Game."

Across earlier chapters, we talked about "demonstrated interest"—the clicks, visits, and responses that feed recruitment systems. For many underrepresented students, that game isn't fair from the start. If you don't have a laptop at home, share a phone, or help manage family responsibilities, you can't show up online the same way as someone with a quiet bedroom and unlimited Wi-Fi.

The danger is that models equate *the amount of engagement with the depth* of interest. A student who signs up for three carefully chosen events and asks thoughtful questions may be *more* serious than a student who auto-registers for everything, but the raw numbers don't always capture that difference. Without safeguards, systems may quietly favor the loudest footprints rather than the strongest fits.

What can you do?

- Students can focus on **high-impact** actions: one or two well-timed virtual sessions, a short but real email to a regional rep, consistent use of the application portal to complete needed steps.
- Parents can help by carving out time and space for those key interactions, even if only once or twice, and by explaining constraints to the college so that human readers understand why your engagement looks the way it does.

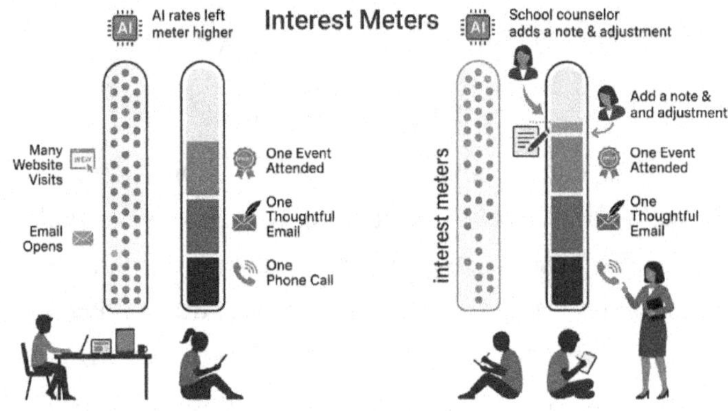

9.4 When Predictive Models Label Students "At Risk."

Colleges also use predictive analytics *after* students enroll—to predict who might be at risk of leaving. Done well, this can help advisors reach out early. Done poorly, it can label underrepresented students in ways that make them feel watched or doubted.

Some patterns to watch:

- Flags based only on grades and logins.
  If a system marks students as "at risk" because of one tough course or a few missed logins, it may flag underrepresented students more often, especially if they are juggling work, commuting, or family duties.
- Support vs. stigma.
  A good system turns a flag into outreach: an advisor email, a tutoring offer, a financial aid check-in. A bad system quietly slots flagged students away from opportunities or treats them as "problems" instead of people.
- One-size-fits-all responses.
  If every "at-risk" student gets the same generic emails, the support may miss what matters: childcare, mental health, food security, or transportation.

If you ever hear that you've been flagged, ask what that means: "What is this based on?" "What support comes with this label?" "How will this affect my opportunities?" Those questions turn a silent risk score into a human conversation.

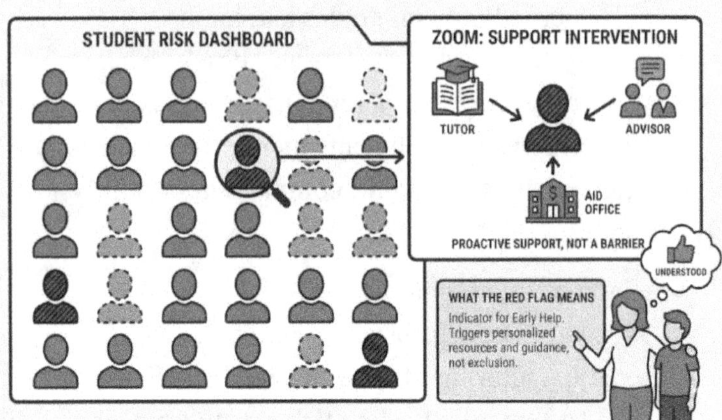

9.5 How AI Can Also Support Underrepresented Students

AI is not automatically against underrepresented students; it simply follows the rules it's given. When people set the right goals, AI can help:

- Finding students in overlooked schools.
  When colleges tell their systems to look for strong students in schools they haven't recruited from before, AI can surface underrepresented students who were never on their radar.
- Identifying equity gaps.
  AI can show where certain groups are missing: "We're not hearing from students in these zip codes" or "Black and Latinx students are less likely to move from inquiry to application." That visibility can push schools to change outreach, not blame students.

- Providing 24/7, judgment-free answers.
  Well-designed chatbots can answer questions that first-generation or low-income students might be hesitant to ask a person: "What if my parents can't help with forms?" "How do I appeal a financial-aid decision?"
- Catching system failures, not just individual struggles.
  Data can reveal patterns: "Many commuter students are dropping this course," or "Students who work 20+ hours a week are missing this deadline." That's a signal to fix course design or policies, not to label those students as failures.

When you see colleges using AI this way—with clear equity goals and human oversight—that's a sign they're trying to turn the technology into a safety net, not a sorting hat.

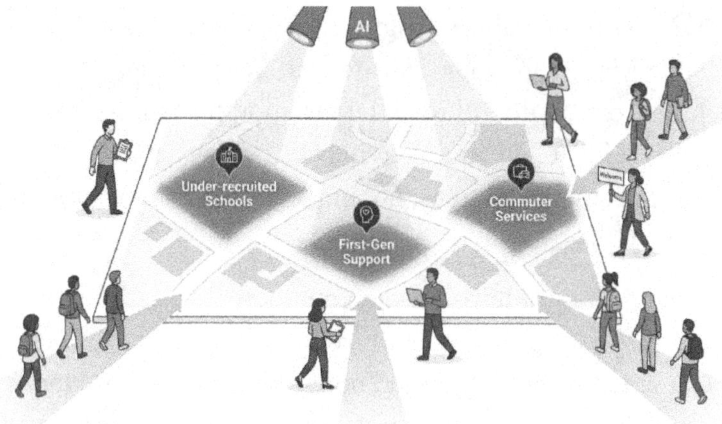

9.6 Key Strategies Families Should Remember (Sidebar)

You can treat this as a boxed summary focused on underrepresented families.

1. Name your reality early
   Use applications, optional questions, and brief emails to share major responsibilities and resource limits. A sentence like "I work 20 hours a week and care for younger siblings, which limits my ability to travel or attend live events," provides readers with critical context.

2. Focus on a few schools, not all of them
   Pick a small set of colleges that fit your academic, financial, and personal needs and invest in those. Underrepresented students don't have endless bandwidth; depth beats scattered activity.

3. Turn invisible strengths into visible signals
   Make sure your real-life work, caregiving, community roles, and translation for family are reflected in your activities list, essays, and recommendations, not hidden behind test scores and GPAs.

4. Ask the equity question out loud
   When you talk to colleges, ask how they use data and technology—and how they prevent those tools from disadvantaging students from under-resourced schools or first-generation backgrounds. You're allowed to ask.

5. Use AI as a translator and planner, not an authority
   Let AI help you decode jargon, organize deadlines, or draft question lists. Don't let it write your story or tell you which colleges are "for people like you." That's your decision.

6. Look for proof, not just promises
   Trust schools that *show* equity work—bridge programs, mentorship, first-gen offices, retention data—not only those that talk about "diversity" in broad terms.

7. Protect your student's bandwidth
   Parents, help your student say no. Not every email, event, or "opportunity" deserves their limited time and energy. Choosing what to skip is as important as choosing what to pursue.

9.7 Student Story: Aaliyah and the "Invisible Interest."

Aaliyah attends a small high school where a four-year college isn't a common path. She works evenings at a grocery store and helps her younger brother with homework. The university she loves is three hours away; campus visits aren't realistic. She worries the college will assume she doesn't care because she can't show up like other students.

With her counselor's help, Aaliyah chooses three high-impact actions:

- She emails her regional admissions counselor to introduce herself, briefly sharing why she's drawn to the school and why travel is hard.
- She registers for one virtual event she can attend and types a specific question into the Q&A about support for working students.
- She regularly logs into her application portal to complete tasks promptly and reads important emails, even if she can't reply to everything.

These steps take time, but not endless hours. They leave a clear trace in the college's systems and, just as important, in the counselor's notes. Aaliyah hasn't changed her circumstances—but she has made sure her genuine interest doesn't stay invisible just because her life is full.

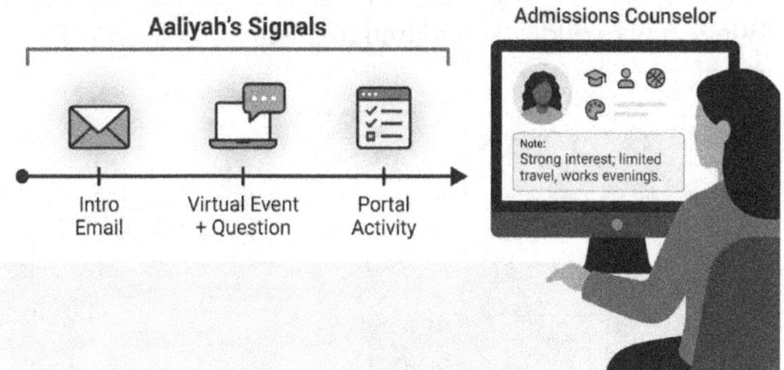

9.8 Parent Story: Mr. Lopez Asks the Hard Question

Mr. Lopez joins a virtual parent session hosted by a private university his daughter is considering. He hears a lot about "personalized outreach," "predictive analytics," and "recruitment dashboards." It all sounds efficient—but he's wondering whether that efficiency really includes students from schools like his daughter's.

During the Q&A, he types: "You mentioned using data and technology in your admissions and recruitment. How do you make sure those tools don't disadvantage students from under-resourced schools or first-generation families?"

The answer he gets shapes his view of the college. If the representative explains how they check bias models, adjust for differences in school resources, and invest in first-generation support, Mr. Lopez feels more comfortable sending his daughter there. If the answer is vague—"We just follow the data"—he notes that down, too. Either way, by asking, he turns AI from a hidden factor into a topic the college has to address in plain language.

9.9 Examples of More Equitable AI-Supported Tools

To make "good AI" less abstract, here are examples of tools and practices that can help underrepresented students instead of hurting them:

1. Equity-focused recruitment dashboards
   These don't just show raw numbers. They highlight who *isn't* being reached—by region, school, first-gen status, or income band—so colleges can send reps, fee waivers, and virtual programming where they've been absent.

2. Context-aware engagement models
   Rather than awarding points only for visits and multiple events, these models recognize that one

email or virtual session from a student at a high-poverty school may equal a full-day visit from a more resourced peer. They adjust the weights accordingly.

3. First-gen and low-income support chatbots
   Some chatbots are designed for a specific audience. They're trained on real questions from first-- and low-income students—about forms, balances, and emergency help—and connect users to human support when issues are complex.

4. Early-alert systems aimed at fixing systems, not students
   Instead of flagging only individuals, these tools highlight patterns: certain courses where underrepresented students struggle disproportionately, or policies that result in repeated late fees for commuters. The "fix" then happens at the course or policy level, not just via warning messages to students.

5. Scholarship matching that surfaces community-based awards
   Better tools don't just push big national scholarships. They elevate local and community-driven awards—faith-based groups, neighborhood foundations, cultural organizations—that often have fewer applicants and stronger ties to underrepresented communities.

6. Transparent explanations for students
   More equitable systems explain, in simple terms,

how certain automated decisions are made and how students can ask for a human review. Even a short "Why you are seeing this" note attached to AI-driven outreach makes the process feel less like a black box.

Should We Add Anything Else Here?

If you want this part of the book to be as useful as possible to underrepresented families, it's worth considering a few additional elements:

- A "Know Your Rights & Options" mini-box
  Briefly outline what students don't have to share with third-party platforms, the right to ask for human review, and the right to ask questions about aid decisions without fear.
- A one-page "Family Conversation Guide."
  Prompts for talking about identity, expectations, comfort with debt, and boundaries around

technology use—so students don't feel they have to carry these decisions alone.

- A myth-busting snapshot
  Quick realities to replace damaging myths like "If we can't visit, we don't have a chance" or "If an algorithm says I'm at risk, that means I don't belong in college."
- A template email that parents or students can customize
  A short, respectful script for asking colleges about their use of AI and their support for first-generation and under-resourced students, ready to paste into an email or message.
- A "What to Look for on College Websites" checklist
  Simple cues—first-gen programs, emergency aid funds, mentoring, transparent outcomes data—that families can scan for when deciding where to invest application energy.

You can decide which of these to include as you refine the manuscript, but all of them share the same goal: turning AI and equity from vague concerns into specific questions families know how to ask and act on.

[Diagram 10 description, blue-and-white palette, icons + humans: A notebook page titled “Add-On Tools for Us.” Bullet icons show “Rights,” “Conversation Guide,” “Myths,” “Template Email,” and “Website Checklist.” A student and parent are seen adding checkmarks next to the ones they want to use, reinforcing that this section is customizable.]

9.10 Checklist for Action: Underrepresented Students

- Write down your full context before you start applications.
- Choose 3–5 colleges to engage with intentionally, instead of trying to engage with all of them.
- Make sure your real-life responsibilities and strengths appear in your applications.

- Ask at least one equity-focused question of any college you seriously consider.
- Use AI tools to understand and organize, not to decide who you are or where you belong.

9.11 Checklist for Action: Parents of Underrepresented Students

- Learn just enough about AI and bias to ask clear questions.
- Practice one or two questions about equity and data before each college meeting or session.
- Help your student prioritize depth over volume in engagement and applications.
- Share your family's story with key people when it adds context that the data can't see.
- Treat colleges as potential *partners*, not just brands—looking for those that show real work on equity, not just nice words.

10 The Parents' Role in an AI-Shaped Admissions Journey

10.1 "Are We Helping or Hijacking?"

By the time junior year turns into senior year, many parents feel two competing instincts pulling at them. On one side is the urge to protect: you see rising costs, confusing technology, and a process that looks nothing like what you went through. On the other side is the desire to step back: you know your student needs to own this journey if they're going to succeed in college when AI is added to the mix—personalized outreach, predictive models, chatbots, and planning tools—that tension gets louder.

The core parenting question in this new landscape isn't just "How do I help?" It's "How do I help *without* taking over?" AI tools can tempt you to manage everything from the kitchen table: sorting emails, filling out forms, even drafting messages. At the same time, the stakes feel high enough that backing off can feel irresponsible. This chapter is about finding a middle path: acting as a steady guide and guardrail while your student remains the driver.

10.2 How AI Changes What Parents See—and Don't See

AI-driven recruitment and admissions change not just what colleges see but also what *you* see as a parent. Compared to previous generations, you may notice:

- More, and more targeted, messages.
  Your student's inbox may be filled with emails mentioning specific majors, locations, or backgrounds. You might receive separate parent-focused messages tailored to your role and zip code.
- Less direct visibility into conversations.
  Students may be chatting with bots, texting reps, or messaging through portals that you don't automatically see, even when those conversations affect their feelings about schools.

- More digital tools that feel "adult" but sit in your teen's hands.
  Net price calculators, AI planners, scholarship-matching tools, and essay checkers all ask for information and make recommendations your student may not fully understand.

That mix can make you feel both over-informed (too many emails, too many dashboards) and under-informed (not sure what your student actually did with those messages or tools). The result is a new kind of anxiety: "Do I jump in—or am I supposed to let them figure this out?"

10.3 The Three Roles Parents Play Now

In an AI-shaped admissions world, parents tend to cycle through three main roles:

- Interpreter
  You help translate complex messages, financial terms, and policy language into clear, understandable ideas. You don't decide, but you

make sure everyone understands what is being decided.

- Organizer
  You help put some structure around a chaotic process—setting up calendars, organizing documents, ensuring important emails don't disappear into spam or get lost in a cluttered inbox.
- Advocate
  You speak up when something doesn't feel fair or clear—whether that's an aid offer that doesn't reflect your reality, a missed outreach to your student's school, or a concern about how data is being used.

The role that *doesn't* work well is "driver." When parents try to run the entire process—choosing schools, managing logins, writing messages- students arrive at college without the skills or ownership they need. AI tools can make it *easier* to slide into the driver's seat because it's simple to log in "for them," answer chat questions, or respond to emails. But ease is not the same as wisdom.

- Interpreter: Parent pointing to a simplified explanation on a tablet.
- Organizer: Parent helping place deadlines on a calendar with the student.
- Advocate: Parent and student together on a video call with a college rep.
  A fourth, crossed-out panel labeled "Driver" shows a parent alone at a laptop with the student faded in the background.

10.4 Healthy Boundaries in a Hyper-Digital Process

When everything runs through devices and accounts, boundaries need to be clearer than ever. Here are practical lines worth drawing early:

- Accounts and logins
  Your student should have their own email and application accounts. You may keep a shared list of logins in a secure place for emergencies, but they

should be the primary user. If you are submitting something on their behalf (for example, a parent's financial portal), clarify what is “theirs” and what is “yours.”

- Voice and authorship
  Your students' essays, activity descriptions, and messages should sound like them. AI tools and parents can help brainstorm and edit, but the final words need to be your student's, not a joint project or a machine's composition.
- Decision thresholds
  Agree as a family on which decisions your student can make independently (for example, registering for virtual events) and which require a conversation (for example, committing to binding programs, sending test scores, or putting down deposits).
- Technology coaching vs. control
  It's appropriate to teach your student how to use AI tools responsibly and to ask about their choices. It's not appropriate to secretly run tools for them or to use technology to monitor every move they make without their knowledge.

Boundaries aren't about withdrawing support; they're about making sure your student learns to navigate complex systems with you beside them, not in front of them.

[Diagram 4 description, blue-and-white palette, icons + humans: A “boundary box” around a student at a laptop. Arrows from the parent come through labeled gates: “Teach,” “Ask,” “Guide.” Arrows labeled “Control,” “Write

For," and "Decide Alone" bounce off the boundary. The parent stands on the outside of the box's edge, close enough to support but not overlapping the student.]

10.5 Talking About AI at the Kitchen Table

AI can be an invisible elephant in the room—everyone's using it or hearing about it, but no one wants to admit it. Bringing it into the open at home is one of the healthiest things you can do. Consider starting with questions like:

- "What AI tools have you used so far—for school or otherwise? What did you like or not like?"
- "What do your friends say about using AI for essays, searching for colleges, or finding scholarships?"
- "Where do you feel AI helps you, and where does it feel like crossing a line?"

As a parent, you can share your own learning curve: "I didn't grow up with this, so I'm still figuring out what's okay and what worries me." That honesty lowers the pressure. You're not interrogating; you're co-learning. From there, you can agree on how AI will and won't be used in your house—for essays, for planning, for research—so your student doesn't feel they have to hide their choices.

You can also talk explicitly about fairness and bias. Ask your student what they've heard about algorithms and underrepresented students. Share any concerns you have about how data might be used. The goal isn't to scare them, but to send a clear message: "If something feels off, we can talk about it and ask questions together."

10.6 Using AI Together as a Planning Assistant

One of the safest and most productive ways to use AI as a family is to treat it as a shared planning assistant. Instead of your student using tools alone in their room or you using them alone when everyone's asleep, set aside time to sit together and ask:

- "Help us build a calendar of key tasks for junior/senior year based on these colleges."
- "Summarize the main differences between these two colleges' cost and aid pages in simple terms."
- "Generate a list of questions we should ask at an upcoming info session about support for first-generation students."

You can paste in text from college websites or emails and let the assistant simplify or organize it. Then you both read the original information and verify the summary together. The assistant is doing the sorting and formatting; you are thinking. This shared use also models *how* to talk to AI tools: be specific, be cautious about what you paste, and use the output as a starting point rather than an answer.

Working side by side like this subtly shifts the dynamic. Instead of the parent always being the human "database" and the student always being the one who asks, both of you are learning how to use new tools for a shared goal. That can lower defensiveness on both sides.

10.7 Financial Scenarios: Who Does What, and With Which Tools?

Money conversations often blur boundaries because parents carry more legal and practical responsibility. AI tools can help here—but only if you're clear about roles.

Scenario A: Comparing Three Colleges' Real Costs

- Student's role: Gather award letters, log into portals, and paste or input information into a comparison tool or assistant.
- Parents' role: Ask an AI assistant (together) to outline differences in grants, loans, and work-study, then check those numbers against the original letters. Raise questions about long-term affordability.

Scenario B: Preparing for a Financial-Aid Appeal

- Student's role: Explain in their own words how they feel about the college and why it's a strong fit.
- Parents' role: Outline financial facts and changed circumstances, then use an AI assistant to help structure a respectful appeal letter. You both review it, edit it into your own voice, and decide who will send it and from which account.

Scenario C: Deciding on Loan Levels

- Student's role: Ask an AI assistant to show what different loan amounts might mean in monthly payments and how those compare to entry-level salaries in their field.
- Parents' role: Bring your experience—mortgages, car payments, other obligations—and talk through what those numbers would feel like in real life. Together, you decide what level of debt the family is comfortable with, or whether a different school or path might be wiser.

In each scenario, the tools do the math and formatting; your family does the values and decisions.

10.8 Guardrails and Agreements: A Family "AI and Admissions" Charter

To keep everyone aligned, many families find it helpful to write down a few simple agreements—a mini "charter" for how you'll handle AI and admissions. It doesn't have to be fancy. It might include statements like:

- "We will be honest about how we use AI in essays and applications."
- "We will use AI to organize and clarify information, not to impersonate or replace anyone's voice."
- "We will talk before sharing sensitive information (like finances) with any new tool or platform."
- "We will respect each other's roles: student leads on content and choices; parents lead on financial reality and safety; AI supports both."

You can revisit this charter as you go. If you're tempted to break a guideline—say, to secretly rewrite an essay or quietly apply your student to a college they haven't approved—it's a signal to pause and talk. The point isn't to police each other; it's to maintain trust in a process where technology could easily become a wedge.

10.9 What Key Strategies Should Parents Remember? (Sidebar)

You can treat this as a quick, parent-focused summary box.

1. Stay in the passenger seat
   Be present, alert, and helpful, but let your student drive decisions where appropriate—especially about essays, applications, and how they present themselves.

2. Talk about AI before it becomes a problem
   Don't wait until you catch your student misusing a tool. Start early with open conversations about what feels ethical, what colleges expect, and how you'll use AI at home.

3. Use tools together when possible
   Sit down with your student to use planners,

comparison tools, and chatbots. It's harder to drift into misuse or misinterpretation when you're working side by side.

4. Ask colleges the hard questions calmly
You're allowed to ask about how they use data, how they protect equity, and what support they offer to first-generation or under-resourced students. Calm, clear questions often get the most honest answers.

5. Protect both privacy and bandwidth
Say no to tools that demand too much personal information. Say no to expectations that your student must respond to every message or attend every event. Boundaries are part of a good strategy.

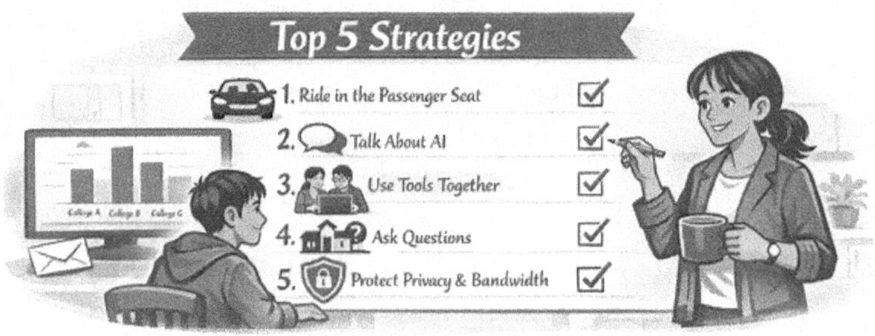

10.10 For Parents of Underrepresented Students: Additional Layers

If your family is underrepresented in higher education, everything in this chapter still applies—but there are extra layers:

- Your student may feel pressure to "prove" themselves in every interaction, which makes healthy boundaries even more important.
- You may feel a stronger urge to protect others because you've seen systems fail people like you before. That's understandable—and it also makes shared decision-making even more crucial.
- AI systems may misread your context, so your advocacy role matters more. This might mean explaining constraints to colleges, asking how they check for bias, and helping your student choose where to invest limited energy.

The key is not to carry all of this alone. Use school counselors, community mentors, cultural organizations, and trusted online resources as part of your support team. AI should expand your access to information, not isolate you.

10.11 Checklist for Action: Parents

- Ask your student how they're already using AI, then listen without judgment.

- Agree on clear roles: where they lead, where you co-decide, and where you take the lead (usually money and safety).
- Schedule a regular "college and AI" check-in—short, predictable, and focused.
- Practice one or two questions you'll ask colleges about their use of data and support for students like yours.
- Write a short family charter for AI and admissions, and revisit it as needed.

10.12 Checklist for Action: Students

- Tell your parents honestly what tools you're using and what you find helpful or confusing.
- Create your own email and application accounts and commit to checking them regularly.
- Keep essays and applications in your own voice, even if you get help brainstorming or editing.
- Invite your parents into planning conversations where their experience matters (costs, logistics), not just at the last minute.
- Speak up if you feel over-managed or under-supported; ask for a different balance rather than shutting down.

11 Building a Digital Presence That Works for You

11.1 Your Online Life Is Part of Your Application (Whether You Want It To Be or Not)

For most teens, the internet is not a "place you visit"; it's where life happens. You post on Instagram, scroll TikTok, chat in group DMs, maybe share art on a portfolio site or code on GitHub. For college admissions, that creates a new reality: long before your application arrives, you already exist online. Colleges may see only a small slice of that—but what they see can reinforce your story, distract from it, or directly contradict it.

This chapter isn't about scaring you into deleting everything. It's about helping you and your parents treat your digital presence the same way you treat your transcript or your essay: as part of the picture. AI-driven tools make it easier for colleges to find public information, and they make it easier for you to organize and shape what's out there. The question is not "Do I have an online footprint?" It's "Does my footprint match who I really am and where I want to go?"

11.2 What Colleges Actually See (and What They Usually Don't)

Let's clear up a big misconception first: most admissions officers are not sitting around doom-scrolling every applicant's feed. They're busy reading transcripts, essays, and recommendations. Surveys and reports suggest that while many colleges think checking social media is "fair game," only a minority routinely do it—and usually when something triggers a look, not as a standard step.

Colleges are more likely to see your digital presence when:

- You link to it yourself in applications (portfolios, YouTube channels, LinkedIn, project sites).
- Your name pulls up something very public in a quick search (articles, local news, a viral post).
- Someone reports concerning content tied to your name or school.

They can't break into private accounts or bypass privacy settings, but they *can* see anything that's public, tagged, or easily searchable. AI-driven tools increasingly help them aggregate public data quickly—such as a basic background search that surfaces public profiles, mentions, or news. That means you don't have to assume they will look; you have to accept that they *might* and act accordingly.

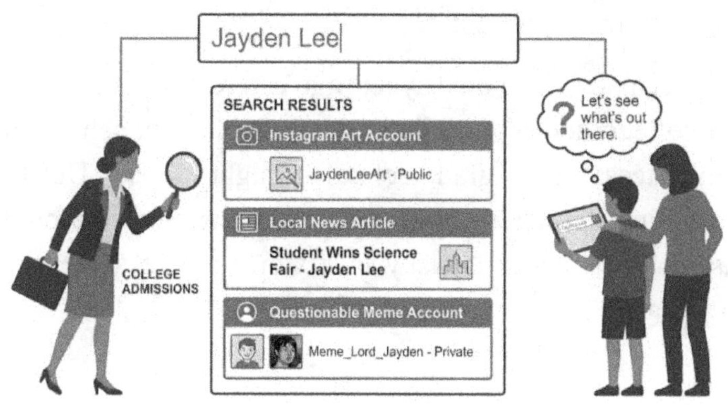

11.3 The Risk Side: When Your Online Life Hurts You

Most of the time, social media doesn't help or hurt you—it's just background noise. But when it does affect admissions, it's more likely to hurt than to help. Public posts that demean others, use slurs, glorify violence, trivialize harm, or show reckless behavior can raise serious character questions. Admissions officers who *do* check social media say they are far more likely to find something that lowers an applicant's chances than something that boosts them.

Common problem areas include:

- Posts or comments that are racist, sexist, homophobic, or otherwise hateful.

- Bullying, harassment, or "jokes" at someone else's expense.
- Content bragging about cheating, substance abuse, or serious rule-breaking.
- Screenshots of private conversations shared publicly without consent.

Even posts you made years ago can resurface. And even if a college doesn't see them now, employers, scholarship committees, and grad schools might later. Deleting everything is not the only answer, but pretending your digital past doesn't matter is risky in a world where screenshots travel fast.

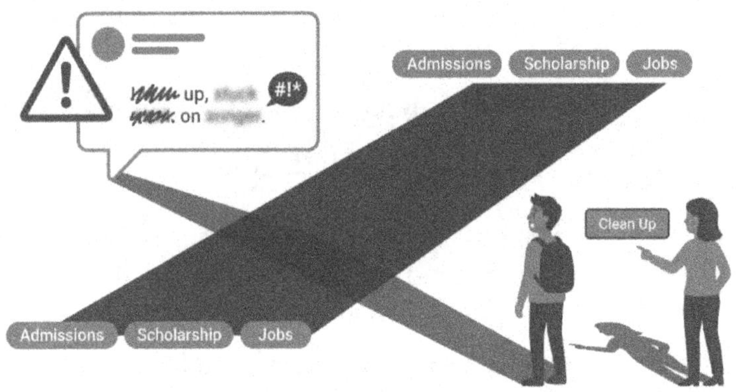

11.4 The Opportunity Side: Turning Your Digital Presence into an Asset

Now, the good news: your online presence can *help* you if it reflects your real passions and projects. Think of it as a living, breathing supplement to your application—not polished like a brochure, but aligned with your story.

Colleges and scholarship providers have shared examples of applicants whose thoughtful online work—like a YouTube channel documenting a science project, an Instagram account showcasing art, or a blog about community organizing—reinforced what they wrote elsewhere and made them more memorable.

A positive digital presence can:

- Show commitment over time (a long-running art page, coding repo, or writing site).
- Demonstrate leadership and initiative (organizing fundraisers, running a small business, creating educational content).
- Offer a deeper look at your voice and values (how you talk about issues, respond to comments, and share your work).

You don't need a huge following or a perfectly curated aesthetic. You need *consistency* between who you say you are on paper and who you appear to be online. That consistency builds trust.

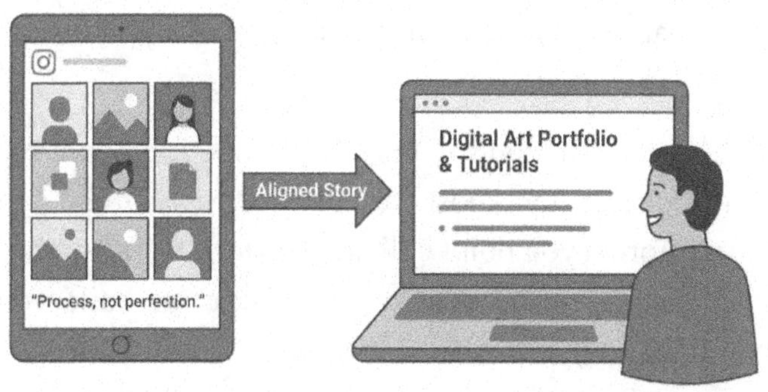

11.5 How AI and Algorithms See You Online

Behind the apps you use, algorithms are constantly deciding what to show you and, in some cases, what to show *about* you. Recommendation systems shape which posts rise to the top of searches or hashtags; AI tools used by marketing teams look at engagement, topics, and network connections to guess your interests or influence. In some corners of enrollment and marketing, colleges (or their vendors) use social and web data to segment audiences and tailor ads or messages.

It's unlikely that an admissions committee is running deep AI scans of every applicant's social presence. But it *is* likely that:

- College marketing teams target posts and ads based on your online behavior or interests.
- Some systems may factor in broad "social footprint" signals (like public profiles linked to your application email) when prioritizing outreach.
- Search and social algorithms may decide what appears first when someone looks up your name or your work.

You can't control those systems fully, but you can control the content most strongly tied to your real name and the platforms you point colleges toward. In other words, you can't control the whole ocean, but you can build your own lighthouse.

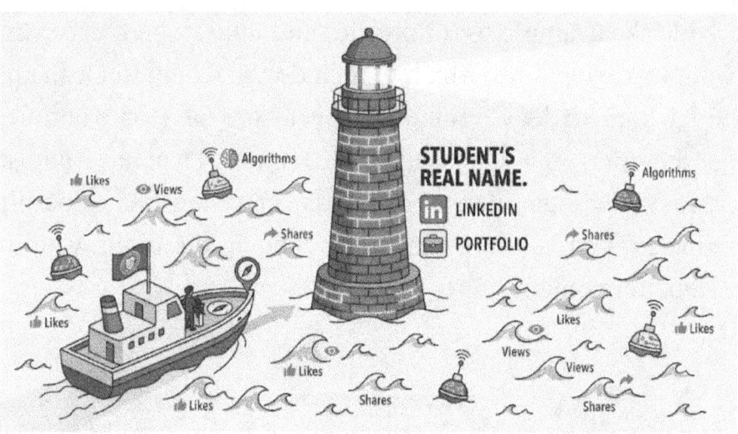

11.6 Step One: Audit Your Digital Footprint Together

The first practical move is simple and slightly uncomfortable: look yourself up.

- Students: Search your name (and common variations) on Google and major social platforms.
- Parents: Sit with your student and do this *together*, not behind their back, so it becomes a shared project, not a secret investigation.

As you scan results, ask:

- "What would a stranger learn about me from this first page of results?"
- "Which profiles are clearly me, and which belong to someone else with my name?"
- "Are there any public posts, photos, or comments that don't match who I am now or who I want to be?"

Make a simple list of profiles and links: which ones you want to keep public, which to lock down, which to clean up, and which to leave alone but be aware of (for example, another person with your same name). Then act: adjust privacy settings, delete or untag anything that doesn't represent you, and note any areas where you might want to add better content.

11.7 Step Two: Decide Which Accounts Are "College-Facing."

You don't have to turn your entire online life into a college brochure. Instead, think about *zones*:

- College-facing zones
  Accounts or sites that you're comfortable having colleges see: a public art or music page, a portfolio, a project blog, a LinkedIn profile, maybe a carefully curated Instagram or YouTube channel.

- Personal zones
  Accounts where you mostly connect with friends and family. These can be more casual but should still avoid anything harmful or hateful, since privacy settings aren't perfect.
- Private zones
  Close friends lists, group chats, or private servers where you can share more freely. Even here, it's wise to remember screenshots exist—but these spaces don't need to be polished or connected to your full real name.

With your parent, decide which accounts fall into each zone. For college-facing accounts, consider using a consistent handle tied to your name and the same email you use for applications. For personal accounts, tighten privacy and be selective about what you make public. For private zones, keep your real name off anything you wouldn't want strangers to see.

11.8 Step Three: Align Your Online Story with Your Offline Story

Colleges aren't looking for perfection; they are looking for coherence. If your application says you're passionate about environmental science, but your public feeds show nothing related—while showcasing a lot of unkind posts or aimless content—that inconsistency can create doubt. On the other hand, if your online presence quietly reinforces the themes in your application, it can strengthen your credibility.

You don't need to post constantly. You might:

- Share occasional updates about projects, performances, competitions, or volunteer work.
- Post behind-the-scenes glimpses: practice sessions, drafts, in-progress builds—not just polished wins.
- Highlight other people's work in your area of interest, showing you're part of a broader community (sharing articles, commenting thoughtfully, amplifying peers).

Parents can help by asking questions like, "If an admissions officer saw this account after reading your application, would it feel like the same person?" and "Is there anything important about you that *doesn't* show up here but could?" Those questions guide, not control.

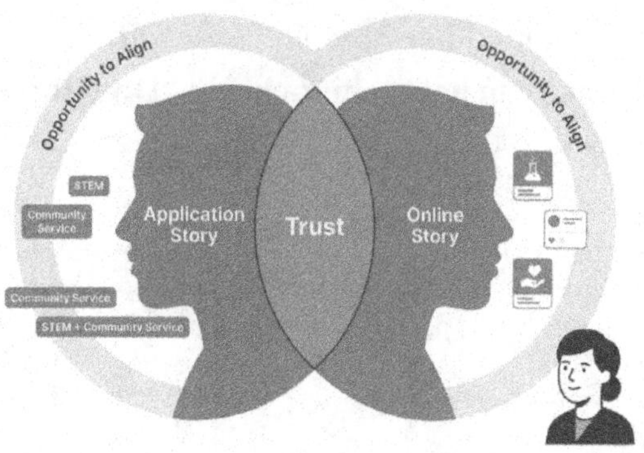

11.9 Using AI to Help Curate and Create (Without Faking It)

AI tools can make managing your digital presence easier—if you keep your voice at the center. Together, you and your parent might use AI to:

- Generate a checklist for a social media clean-up ("What should I review on my public profiles before applying to college?").
- Summarize your existing online projects into a short bio for a portfolio or LinkedIn ("Summarize these activities into a 2–3 sentence description.").
- Brainstorm content ideas that match your interests ("What are some post ideas to show my interest in theater/robotics/healthcare?").

Crucially, you should edit any AI-generated text into your own words before posting. AI can help you organize thoughts, but if you let it write your captions or bios completely, you risk sounding generic or unlike yourself. The goal is to sound like *you on a good day*, not like a press release. Parents can help sanity-check: "Does this sound like how you talk?"

11.10 For Underrepresented Students: Owning Your Story Online

If you're underrepresented in higher education, your digital presence can be a powerful way to show parts of your story that transcripts and test scores often miss. That might include:

- Translating for family or organizing in your community.
- Working jobs that show responsibility and grit.
- Being active in cultural, faith-based, or advocacy spaces.

You can choose how much of this to share publicly, but know that these experiences are *assets*, not things to hide. A short thread about what you've learned from balancing school and work, or a post highlighting a community project, can underscore themes you bring into essays. Just be sure you're sharing from a place of pride and safety, not pressure.

Parents can support by affirming that these parts of the student's life *count* and by helping set boundaries around privacy and security, especially when posts involve other family members or sensitive topics.

11.11 Quick Wins: What Students Can Do This Month

Think of these as realistic, one-month goals, not a life overhaul.

- Google yourself and list what appears on the first page.
- Lock down or clean up at least one personal account.
- Choose one platform to be your "college-facing" space and make sure your name and basic info are clear and professional.

- Share one authentic post related to your interests, projects, or community involvement.
- Ask a trusted adult to quickly scroll your main public profile and tell you what they see first—then decide if that matches what you want.

11.12 Quick Wins: Parents Can Now

Parents can take parallel steps without taking control:

- Ask your student if you can do a digital audit *together,* then follow their lead.
- Offer to help with privacy settings and basic clean-up, but let your student decide what to keep or share, as long as it's safe and respectful.
- Encourage your student to create or update one college-facing profile (LinkedIn, portfolio, or a focused public account) rather than pushing them to polish everything.
- Learn the basics of how colleges view social media so you can give accurate guidance, not just "delete everything and disappear."
- Reinforce that their online presence should reflect *who they are,* not who they think admissions wants them to pretend to be.

12 Using AI Tools Responsibly in the Application Process

12.1 The New Question: "How Much AI Is Too Much?"

By now, you've seen AI show up in nearly every part of the journey: college search tools, scholarship matchers, chatbots, and planning apps. When you finally sit down to work on applications, it's natural to wonder, "Can I use AI here too—and if so, how far is too far?"

This chapter treats AI like what it *should* be in the application phase: a helpful assistant in the background, not the author of your story or the decision-maker for your future. We'll walk through concrete examples—good and bad—then spell out clear dos and don'ts that students and parents can refer back to when the pressure ramps up.

12.2 Where AI Fits in the Application Workflow

Think of the application process as a series of stages:

1. Planning and organizing
2. Researching and comparing schools
3. Brainstorming essays and short answers
4. Drafting and revising writing
5. Filling forms and tracking deadlines
6. Preparing for interviews or conversations

AI can play a positive role at almost every stage—except one: it must not replace you when it's time to produce your *actual* answers and stories. Here's a quick map:

- Strong fit for AI Planning timelines, making checklists, summarizing information, generating practice questions, brainstorming topics, spotting repeated phrasing, and simplifying complex instructions.
- Caution or "no-go" zone: Writing full essays or short answers, inventing stories or experiences, choosing colleges *for* you, submitting text you could never reasonably recreate on your own.

If you're ever unsure, one test works almost every time: if an admissions officer asked you to sit in a room and hand-write a version of what you submitted, could you produce something recognizably similar? If not, AI has done too much.

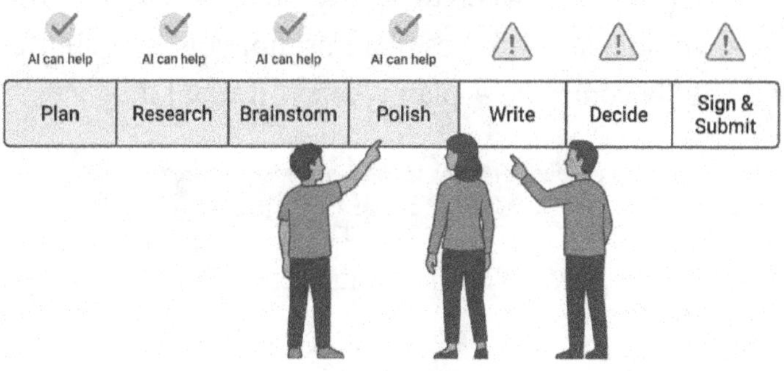

12.3 Example: Using AI to Plan Without Taking Over

Imagine you're a junior heading into the fall. You know there are essays, recommendation requests, test dates, and various college deadlines coming, but it all feels like a blur. You and a parent sit down and ask an AI assistant:

- "Help us create a month-by-month application timeline for a student applying to 6–8 colleges, with most deadlines on January 1."

The assistant suggests general milestones, including when to finalize your college list, request recommendations, draft essays, and complete forms. You then adjust those dates to match the actual deadlines on each college's website and your personal calendar—moving tasks around exams, sports seasons, or family obligations. The AI gave you a starting structure, but you made the final plan.

What you *don't* do is ask, "What colleges should I apply to?" and unquestioningly accept whatever list comes back, or "Tell me exactly when to do everything," and then ignore your own schedule. AI sees patterns, not your unique life. Its plan only becomes *your* plan when you adapt it.

12.4 Example: Brainstorming Essays vs. Letting AI Write Them

Scenario A (Responsible Use): You type: "Ask me 10 questions to help me brainstorm topics for a personal statement about growth, resilience, or curiosity. Don't write anything for me—ask questions."

The AI responds with prompts like:

- "Tell me about a time you faced a challenge and how you responded."
- "What's something you've stuck with even when it was hard?"

You answer these questions in your own words, jotting notes in a document or notebook. From those answers, you choose one story that feels meaningful and start a first draft *without* any AI text. Later, once you have a full draft, you might ask, "Show me sentences that are confusing or repetitive." You review the suggestions, keep the ones that still sound like you, and ignore the rest.

Scenario B (Crossing the Line): You type: "Write a 650-word college essay about overcoming challenges as a first-generation student who works part-time and wants to study biology." You paste the AI's output into your application and only change a few words.

In Scenario B, the essay may sound smooth—but it's not your voice, and you didn't do the heavy lifting of reflecting and crafting. It also increases the chance that your essay sounds eerily similar to others who used the same prompt. That's exactly the kind of thing that raises red flags.

12.5 Example: Using AI on Activity Lists and Short Answers

The activities section and small response boxes are where students often feel the tightest squeeze. How do you capture a whole job, club, or family responsibility in 150 characters?

Responsible use might look like this:

- You write a rough, longer description of what you do in an activity.

- You tell an AI assistant: "Help me shorten this to about 150 characters while keeping the meaning. Don't add anything new."
- It suggests a shorter version. You check it for accuracy, adjust words to match your voice, and tweak details.

Or you might say: "Here are three ways I described this job. Which one is clearest and most specific?" The tool compares them, and you pick the one that best fits.

Crossing the line would look more like: "Write a powerful description of my volunteering that makes me sound like a hero," and then pasting whatever appears without caring if it accurately reflects what you actually did. The moment AI starts exaggerating, embellishing, or adding flair you didn't live, it's working against your honesty.

12.6 Example: Preparing for Interviews With AI as Your Practice Partner

Many students are nervous about interviews—whether they're formal alum interviews, conversations with admissions reps, or more casual chats at college fairs. AI can be a low-pressure practice partner:

- You ask: "Give me 10 common college interview questions and follow-up questions."
- You practice answering out loud, maybe even recording yourself.

- You ask: "Based on this sample answer, what questions should I be ready to answer next?"

The key is that you're using the prompts to *rehearse*, not to memorize scripted answers. A real interview is a conversation, not a performance. Parents can use these same prompts to practice listening and asking follow-up questions at home, turning the dinner table into a no-stakes practice zone.

What you *don't* want to do is copy AI-generated answers verbatim onto notecards and read them back like a script. Interviewers can hear when responses sound canned or generic. It's better to stumble a little in your own words than to speak flawlessly with no real connection.

12.7 Do and Don't Lists: AI and Essays

Do:

- Do write a full first draft without any AI text.

- Do use AI to ask you reflection questions that help you dig deeper into your own experiences.
- Do ask for help spotting confusing sentences or repeated wording, then decide which suggestions to accept.
- Do keep versions of your drafts, so you can show your writing process if anybody ever asks.
- Do read your essay out loud to someone who knows you and ask, "Does this sound like me?"

Don't:

- Don't ask AI to write full essays or major sections for you.
- Don't let AI "translate" your ideas into a voice that doesn't sound like your own speaking or writing.
- Don't paste AI text into your application without thorough, honest revision in your own words.
- Don't rely on AI to invent stories, hardships, or achievements; it's both unethical and easily detectable through inconsistency.
- Don't ignore that some colleges now ask directly about AI use; assume they care about how you've used these tools.

12.8 Do and Don't Lists: AI and Forms, Portals, and Logistics

Do:

- Do use AI to create personal checklists from long instructions ("Summarize what I need to do from this email.").
- Do ask AI to explain confusing terms in forms (like "superscore," "CSS Profile," or "noncustodial parent") in simpler language, then confirm details with official sources.
- Do ask for help organizing deadlines into a calendar or timeline format.
- Do let AI remind you of common items needed for applications (transcripts, test scores, recommendation requests) so you don't forget basics.

Don't:

- Don't let AI autofill sensitive forms or financial information into external tools—you should input those yourself on official college or government sites.
- Don't rely solely on AI summaries of requirements; always double-check actual instructions on the college or scholarship website.
- Don't paste entire legal or financial forms into unknown tools; maintain a boundary around sensitive data.
- Don't allow AI to create accounts or submit anything on your behalf.

12.9 Do and Don't Lists: Parents Using AI in the Application Phase

Do:

- Do use AI to help decode complex admissions or financial-aid language into simpler terms that you and your student can discuss.
- Do use tools together with your student when planning timelines, comparing costs, or brainstorming questions for admissions or financial-aid staff.
- Do model ethical behavior by being honest about any AI assistance you use, especially on letters or appeals that come from you.
- Do ask AI to help you prepare for conversations ("What should I ask a financial-aid officer about our special circumstances?") while you keep the actual story personal and specific.

Don't:

- Don't secretly use AI to write your students' essays, short answers, or emails to colleges.
- Don't let AI drive your student's college list without considering fit, finances, and your student's actual feelings.
- Don't treat AI output as "official"; always verify with human experts—counselors, college reps, or financial-aid officers—especially on money questions.

- Don't use AI tools as a replacement for talking with your student; use them as a reason to sit down and talk *more.*

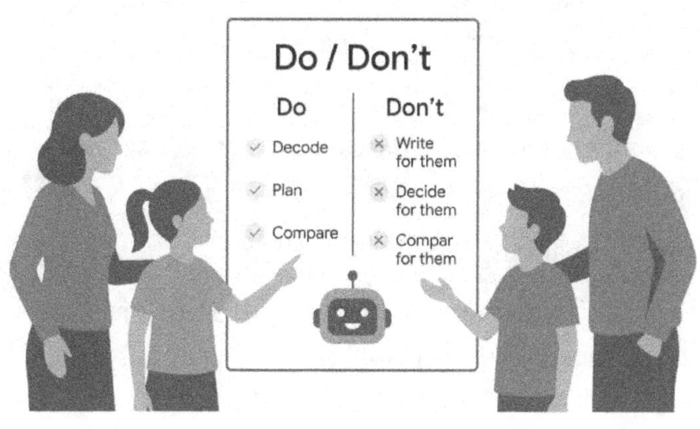

12.10 More Concrete Scenarios: "Is This Okay?"

Scenario 1: Copy-editing vs. Rewriting

- You write an essay draft and ask AI: "Check for grammar and punctuation only. Don't change my wording."
- It suggests fixing a few commas and verb tenses. You accept those changes.

Verdict: OK. You still did the conceptual and stylistic work; the tool functioned like a spell-checker.

Scenario 2: Style Makeover

- You paste your draft in and ask: "Rewrite this in a more sophisticated style with more advanced vocabulary."
- The new version sounds like a middle-aged professor, not a teenager.

Verdict: Not OK. You've replaced your voice with a manufactured one. You can ask for clarity, not for a new persona.

Scenario 3: Activity List Help

- You write: "I tutor my little brother and two neighbors in math and reading after school," then ask AI: "Shorten this to ~100 characters without adding anything."

Verdict: OK, as long as the final version is accurate and still sounds like something you'd say.

Scenario 4: "Tell Me What to Say" Emails

- Before emailing an admissions rep, you ask AI: "Give me a template email to ask about visiting campus and financial-aid info."
- You then customize it heavily with details about your situation and questions that truly matter to you.

Verdict: OK. Templates are starting points, not final products.

Scenario 5: Recommendation Letters

- A teacher or parent asks AI to draft a recommendation "to save time" and signs it without major changes.

Verdict: Risky and often not appropriate. Recommendations are meant to be in the recommender's voice; if AI is used at all, it should be for structure or bullet-point organization, not full writing.

12.11 Additional Examples: Good vs. Problematic AI Prompts

You can use this as a quick reference table in your drafting:

- Better prompt:
  "Ask me questions to help me reflect on experiences that shaped my interest in engineering. Do not write an essay."
- Risky prompt:
  "Write a compelling essay about my passion for engineering using vivid detail and emotional language."
- Better prompt:
  "Here is my own 300-word paragraph. Help me organize it into a clearer structure with an introduction, middle, and conclusion."
- Risky prompt:
  "Rewrite this so it sounds more impressive and professional and uses big words."
- Better prompt:
  "Summarize this financial-aid email in plain language and list the actions I need to take."

- Risky prompt:
  "Tell me if this aid package is good or bad and whether I should choose this college."

Remember: the safer prompts keep the thinking, deciding, and storytelling in *your* hands.

12.12 Checklist for Action: Students

- List all the AI tools you're currently using (or thinking about) for applications and label what you're using them for (planning, writing, organizing, etc.).
- For each tool, ask: "Is this helping me think and organize, or is it starting to do the work *for* me?" Adjust as needed.
- Commit to writing first drafts of essays and short answers without AI text, even if you brainstorm with AI questions.
- Before submitting, pick one trusted person (teacher, counselor, parent) to read your writing and confirm that it sounds like you.
- Keep a simple log of how you've used AI during the process so you can explain it honestly if a college ever asks.

12.13 Checklist for Action: Parents

- Talk with your student about where they're using AI now and where they feel unsure about what's okay.
- Agree together on red lines: no AI-written essays, no AI deciding the college list alone, no sharing of sensitive data with unknown tools.
- Offer to sit with your student when using AI for planning or decoding complex information, so you can both learn how to use it wisely.
- Use AI only to support your own tasks (like understanding aid letters), never to secretly write or rewrite your student's application content.
- Reassure your student that their honest, imperfect voice is more valuable than a polished but generic AI-generated version.

13 What Admissions Officers Want You to Know About AI

13.1 "We Know You're Using It."

If you could listen in on admissions meetings right now, you'd hear something like this: "We know students are using AI. The question is how." Admissions officers are not naïve. They understand that AI has become part of school, work, and daily life. Many use similar tools themselves to draft emails, organize data, or plan outreach.

What worries them is not that you *ever* touched an AI tool. What worries them is when AI starts to erase your voice, blur the truth, or make applications feel interchangeable. This chapter translates what many admissions professionals say behind closed doors into kitchen-table language you and your family can use.

13.2 How Admissions Officers Actually Read Applications Now

Before we talk about AI specifically, it helps to understand the rhythm of how applications are read:

- Time is tight
  Many officers read dozens of files per day. They don't have time to run deep investigations on every sentence. They're looking for a clear, honest sense of who you are and whether you fit what the college offers.
- They read across the whole file
  Essays are not evaluated in isolation. Officers compare your main essay, short responses, activity list, recommendations, and sometimes graded writing samples. They're listening for a consistent voice and story.
- They work in teams
  Often, at least two people will see your application. In some places, a committee reviews borderline cases. That means more than one person may notice weird or inconsistent elements.

AI hasn't changed these core habits. What has changed is the *range* of writing styles they see and the *frequency* with which things feel oddly polished or generic.

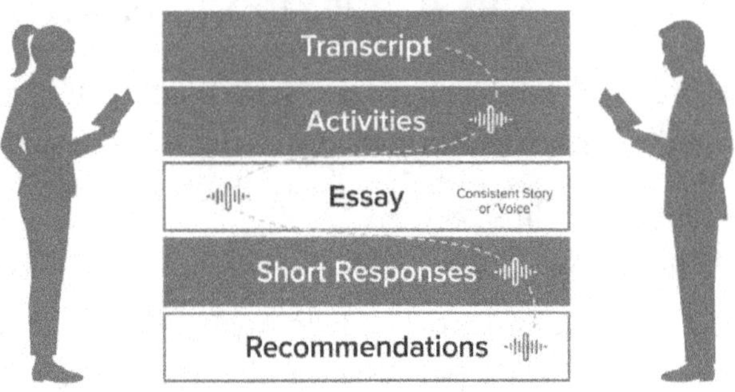

13.3 What Admissions Officers Say They Want (On the Record)

When asked publicly, many admissions officers repeat similar themes about AI and applications:

- Authenticity over perfection
  They would rather read a slightly messy essay that sounds like a real teenager than a flawless essay that sounds like a brochure.
- Transparency over secrecy
  If a college asks about AI use, they want honest answers—how you used it, where you drew the line. They're more concerned about dishonesty than about moderate, disclosed assistance.
- Ownership over outsourcing
  They want to feel that *you* did the key thinking: choosing topics, reflecting on experiences, deciding

what matters. Tools and helpers (including adults) should play a supporting role, not be in charge.

Behind those themes is a simple reality: colleges admit *students*, not AI tools, not parents, not consultants. They're trying to evaluate whether the student who shows up on campus will be ready to write, think, struggle, and grow.

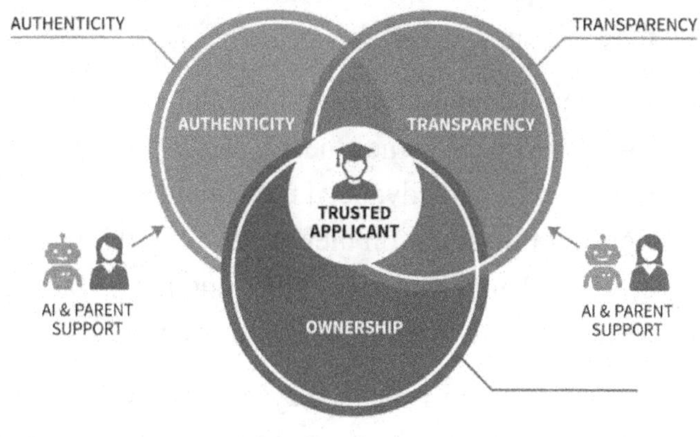

13.4 What They Worry About (Behind the Scenes)

In conversation, admissions officers often voice specific worries about AI use:

- "Same-sounding" essays
  They're seeing more essays with similar structure, tone, and phrases—even from students in different regions and schools. It can feel like reading variations of the same piece over and over.
- Voice mismatch
  They see polished essays that sound far more

advanced than the student's short responses, activity descriptions, or writing samples. That mismatch raises questions about who really wrote what.

- Over-helpful adults
  They worry that AI has become one more way for adults—parents, tutors, consultants—to take over the process, leaving them unsure whose work they're actually evaluating.
- Uneven access
  They know that some students have high-priced human help and advanced tools, while others are figuring things out on their own. They worry that AI could widen gaps if it becomes another advantage for families with more time and resources.

These worries don't mean they're anti-AI. They mean they are trying to protect the integrity of the process and make good decisions with limited time and imperfect information.

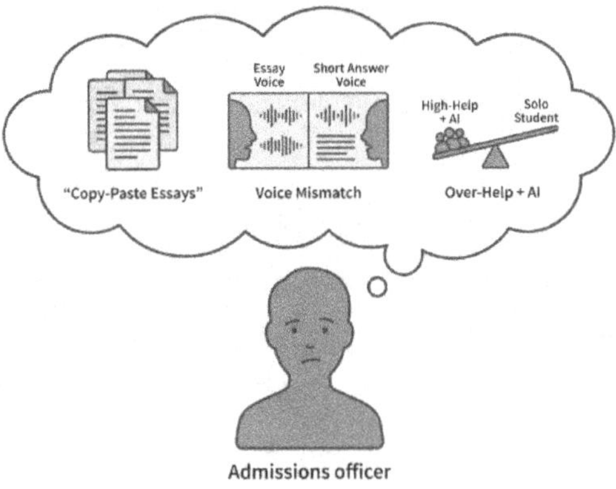

13.5 How Some Colleges Are Setting AI Rules

Policies vary by campus, but you'll see a few common approaches emerging:

- "No AI writing" policies
  Some colleges explicitly state that students must write essays and short answers without generative tools. They may allow basic spelling or grammar checkers, but draw a firm line at content generation.
- "Limited, disclosed use" policies
  Others allow students to use AI for brainstorming, organizing, or light editing, as long as the student maintains control and is honest if asked. They focus on intent and degree rather than banning tools outright.
- "Honor code" extensions
  Many colleges tie AI use to existing honor codes or academic integrity policies, emphasizing that misrepresenting AI-generated work as your own is a form of plagiarism or cheating.
- "We're still figuring it out."
  Some institutions are openly in transition. They may not have detailed written policies yet, but individual officers are watching closely for overuse and discussing internally where to draw lines.

Because the landscape is shifting, it's wise to look for AI guidelines on each college's admissions website and to ask directly on tours or in info sessions, "Do you have a policy about using AI when working on applications?"

13.6 Q&A: What Admissions Officers Wish They Could Tell Every Family

You can imagine this as a "myth-busting" conversation.

Q: "If my essay isn't perfect, will you think I'm not prepared for college?"
A: No. We know you're still in high school. We want to see that you can communicate clearly and think about your experiences. A few rough edges are fine; an artificial voice is not.

Q: "If I admit I used AI to brainstorm or check grammar, will that hurt me?"
A: Generally, no—if you stayed in control and did your own writing. We'd rather you be honest about the light support you received than pretend you did everything alone.

Q: "Can you always tell if someone used AI?"
A: Not always. But we can often tell when something doesn't sound like a teenager, or doesn't sound like the same person across the application. That triggers questions and sometimes further review.

Q: "Do you secretly prefer AI-polished essays because they're easier to read?"
A: We prefer essays that feel like *you*. Highly polished but

generic pieces blur together. Specific, honest, human essays stand out—even if they're less smooth.

Q: "Should I mention AI in my application?"
A: Only if the college asks or if it's necessary to explain your process. If you do, be concise and concrete: what you used it for, where you stopped, and how you made sure the final work was yours.

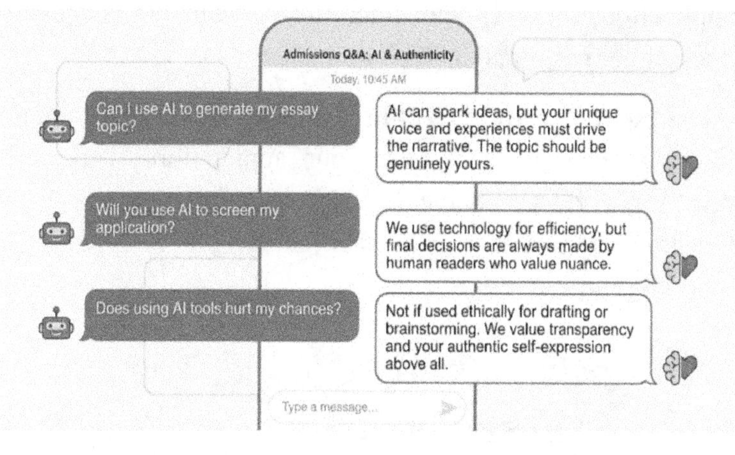

13.7 Insider-Style Scenario: The Essay That Felt "Copied and Pasted from the Internet."

An admissions officer reads a technically flawless essay—excellent vocabulary, elegant structure, smooth transitions. But something is off. The content is vague, filled with phrases such as "ever since I was a child" and "this transformative journey has shaped who I am today," and offers few concrete details. Later, the officer reads the student's short answers: they're brief, direct, and full of specific, down-to-earth language.

The officer flags the file for a second reader with a note: "Essay feels generic and not in the same voice as the rest." The second reader agrees. They don't have proof of heavy AI use, but the mismatch weakens their confidence that the essay reflects the student. When it's time to rank the application, they still consider the student, but the essay doesn't help as much as it could have.

Takeaway: An over-polished essay that doesn't sound like you can actually *hurt* your application. It doesn't necessarily get you denied—but it misses the chance to be the strongest part of your file.

13.8 Insider-Style Scenario: The Messy Essay That Stuck with the Committee

Another officer reads an essay that starts with an imperfect, slightly awkward sentence—but immediately offers a vivid snapshot: a student closing up a restaurant after a late shift, balancing homework on the bus ride home, and reflecting on what they've learned from managing responsibility. The vocabulary is simple. There are a few repeated words. But the voice is unmistakably human and specific.

In committee, when files blur together, someone says, "Remember the student who wrote about doing algebra problems at the bus stop after work?" Heads nod. That essay becomes shorthand for a real, three-dimensional person. When the committee weighs borderline cases, the clarity of that story—and its alignment with the activity list and recommendations—tips the conversation toward "admit."

Takeaway: A clear, specific story in your voice can matter more than flawless prose. Committees remember people, not phrases.

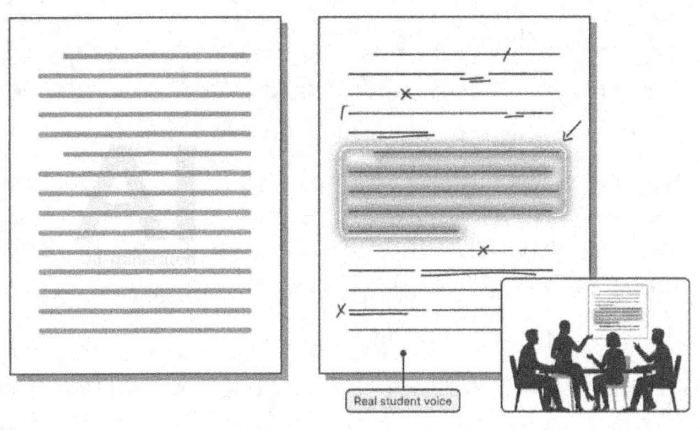

13.9 Underrepresented Students: What Admissions Officers Are Trying (and Sometimes Failing) to Do

Many admissions officers are acutely aware that underrepresented students—by race, income, geography, or first-generation status—are navigating AI from a different starting line. They're trying to balance:

- Not penalizing students who don't have access to consultants or extensive adult help.

- Not rewarding polished AI-assisted work more than genuine but less polished writing from students with fewer supports.
- Using predictive tools to extend opportunity rather than shrink it.

Some are actively revising their rubrics to prioritize context and substance over surface polish. They may put more weight on recommendations, activities, and evidence of persistence than on essay "style points." They may pay close attention to how underrepresented students describe obstacles and support systems, knowing that these are often undercaptured in data.

But they're also human, working within imperfect systems. That's why your clarity about context—work, caregiving, school resources, internet access—can help them read your application in a fuller, fairer way. They can't fix every algorithm, but they *can* advocate more effectively when they understand your reality.

13.10 Concrete Advice from the Admissions Side: Students

Here is how many admissions officers would coach you if they were sitting at your kitchen table:

- "Write as you talk on your best day."
  Not how you talk with your closest friends, not how you talk in a rushed text. How you talk when you're explaining something that matters to a trusted adult.

- "Show us one or two real stories; don't try to cram your whole life into 650 words."
  Specific moments beat general summaries.
- "If you use AI, use it early in the process, not late."
  Brainstorming questions and organization prompts are safer than last-minute rewriting.
- "Let us see how you think, not just what you've done."
  Use essays and short answers to show reflection: what changed you, what you learned, what surprised you.
- "Trust that we can handle your real voice."
  You don't need to sound like a professor. You need to sound like a thoughtful high-school student who is ready for the next step.

13.11 Concrete Advice from the Admissions Side: Parents

If admissions officers could send one private memo to parents, it might sound like this:

- "We want to hear your student's voice, not yours or a bot's."
  Help them brainstorm. Talk through ideas. But when you're tempted to rewrite, step back and ask, "Does this sound like them?"
- "Your advocacy is welcome; your authorship is not."
  It's appropriate for you to write letters or emails that come from *you* (about finances, context, or questions). It's not appropriate to ghost-write what's supposed to be your student's work.
- "We understand you're worried about fairness."
  If you're concerned about how AI or data might affect underrepresented students, ask us. Calm, direct questions help us see where we need to be clearer and fairer.
- "If your student tells us they did everything alone, but we can tell adults or tools did a lot, that hurts trust."
  Help them be honest about the support they had, and help them keep that support within reasonable limits.
- "We still want to see struggle, not just polish."
  College will challenge your student. We need to

know they can handle hard thinking and imperfect conditions, not just externally smoothed edges.

13.12 A Simple Framework: "Think – Draft – Check – Reflect."

To keep AI in its proper place, families can use a four-step framework:

1. Think
   Student reflects (alone or with others) on experiences, values, and goals. AI may ask questions, but does not yet suggest content.
2. Draft
   Students write first drafts of major components (essays, short answers, activity descriptions) in their own words, without AI rewriting.

3. Check
   Students may use AI to:
   - Clarify instructions
   - Summarize requirements
   - Point out confusing or repetitive sections
   - Suggest clearer phrasing *within* the student's style

The student decides which suggestions to accept.

4. Reflect
   Student and, when appropriate, parent or counselor, read the final version and ask:
   - "Does this sound like you?"
   - "Does it feel honest?"
   - "Could you recreate this if you needed to?"

If the answer to those questions is yes, you're likely on safe ground with admissions officers.

13.13 Checklist for Action: Students

- Read your main essay and short answers out loud. If you wouldn't say those sentences in real life, revise until you would.
- Make a list of where you plan to use AI (if at all) and why—brainstorming, organizing, checking clarity—then stick to that plan.
- Look up at least one college's statement or FAQ about AI use in applications so you understand their expectations.
- Ask one adult who knows your writing (teacher, counselor) to tell you honestly whether your application sounds like your past work.
- Be prepared to explain, in one or two sentences, how you used AI in the process if someone asks.

13.14 Checklist for Action: Parents

- Have an explicit conversation with your student about what is and isn't okay for AI and adult help on applications.
- Decide on one clear family rule—for example, "AI can help brainstorm and check grammar, but can't write paragraphs we'll submit."
- Ask admissions reps at least one question about how their institution is approaching AI and academic integrity.

- Resist the urge to "polish away" your student's natural voice; if you're not sure, ask a third party if the essay still sounds like your student.
- Reassure your student that colleges expect growth and learning, not finished products—AI is not the secret key to admission; authenticity and fit still matter most.

When families understand what admissions officers are really looking for—and what makes them uneasy—AI becomes less of a mystery and more of a manageable tool. You don't have to guess what they think; you can align your choices with the values they're actually trying to uphold.

14 Workbook

14.1 Yes, You Have Homework!

Comprehensive Workbook Series: AI's Impact on College Recruitment

Student Workbook: Your AI-Powered College Journey

Introduction: How to Use This Workbook

This workbook is your companion as you navigate college recruitment in an AI-driven world. Each section corresponds to a chapter in the main book and includes reflection questions, practical exercises, checklists, and planning tools. Work through these at your own pace, revisit sections as needed, and use the space to organize your thoughts and strategy.

What You'll Need:

- This workbook
- Access to a computer or phone with internet
- A calendar or planner
- Honest conversations with trusted adults

Chapter 1 Workbook: How Colleges Use AI to Find You

Exercise 1.1: Understanding Your Digital Trail

Trace Your Visibility

List every place where colleges might "see" you digitally:

1. Test registration sites (SAT/ACT/other):
   - Date registered: _______________
   - Information shared: _______________
2. College Board Student Search Service or similar (check if applicable):
   - ☐ Yes, I opted in
   - ☐ No, I opted out
   - ☐ I don't know
3. College websites I've visited in the past 6 months:
   - ____
   - ____
   - ____
4. Virtual events or webinars I've attended:
   - ____
   - ____
5. Email addresses where I receive college mail:
   - ____

Reflection Questions:

1. Were you aware that visiting a college website might trigger a recruitment contact?

____

2. How do you feel knowing colleges are building profiles based on your digital activity?

3. What surprised you most about how colleges find students?

Exercise 1.2: Audit Your Inbox

College Email Analysis

Over the next week, track the college emails you receive:

Date	College Name	Subject Line	Did I Open It?	Did It Feel Personalized?	Action Taken
			☐ Yes ☐ No	☐ Yes ☐ No	
			☐ Yes ☐ No	☐ Yes ☐ No	
			☐ Yes ☐ No	☐ Yes ☐ No	
			☐ Yes ☐ No	☐ Yes ☐ No	
			☐ Yes ☐ No	☐ Yes ☐ No	

Analysis:

1. What percentage of emails did you actually open? ________%

2. Which subject lines caught your attention most?

---

3. Did any emails mention specific details about you (location, major interest, activities)?

---

4. Which colleges should you follow up with based on genuine interest?

Exercise 1.3: Taking Control

Create Your Communication Strategy

Email Organization Plan:

1. I will check college emails:
   - ☐ Daily
   - ☐ Every other day
   - ☐ Twice a week
   - ☐ Weekly

Specific day/time: _______________

2. I will create folders/labels for:
   - ☐ High-interest colleges
   - ☐ Medium-interest colleges
   - ☐ Not interested

   - ☐ Scholarship opportunities
   - ☐ Important deadlines
3. For colleges I'm genuinely interested in, I will:
   - ☐ Open their emails regularly
   - ☐ Visit their website
   - ☐ Attend at least one virtual event
   - ☐ Follow on social media
   - ☐ Other: _______________

Boundary Setting:

I will unsubscribe from college emails when:

- **Action Checklist: Chapter 1**
- ☐ I've identified all the places where I've shared my information with colleges
- ☐ I've set up an email organization system for college communications
- ☐ I've created a schedule for checking and responding to college outreach
- ☐ I've talked with a parent or counselor about my communication strategy

- ☐ I understand that I control how much engagement I show

Completion Date: _______________

Chapter 2 Workbook: Understanding Algorithmic Profiling

Exercise 2.1: What Data Points Define You?

Your Profile as the Algorithm Sees It

Fill in what colleges likely know about you through data:

Academic Profile:

- GPA range: _______________
- Test scores (if applicable): _______________
- Courses taken: _______________
- Academic interests: _______________

Geographic Profile:

- Zip code: _______________
- School name: _______________
- Region: ☐ Urban ☐ Suburban ☐ Rural
- Distance from colleges you're interested in: _______________

Engagement Profile:

- Number of college websites visited in past 3 months: _______________

- Virtual events attended: _______________
- Campus visits (if any): _______________
- Email open rate (estimate): _______________

Demographic Profile (what you've shared):

- Intended major interest: _______________
- First-generation status: ☐ Yes ☐ No ☐ Prefer not to say
- Other information shared: _______________

- **Exercise 2.2: Beyond the Data**

What the Algorithm Doesn't Know

List 5 important things about you that wouldn't show up in an algorithmic profile:

1. ______________________________
2. ______________________________
3. ______________________________
4. ______________________________
5. ______________________________

Reflection:

How can you make sure these "invisible" parts of your story become visible in your applications?

____

____

____

____

- **Exercise 2.3: Strategic Profile Building**

Intentional Engagement Plan

For your top 3–5 colleges, plan how you'll show genuine interest:

College 1: ______________________________

Actions I'll take:

- ☐ Attend virtual info session (date: _______________)
- ☐ Request information from the website
- ☐ Connect with admissions rep (name: _______________)
- ☐ Visit campus (if possible) (date: _______________)
- ☐ Follow on social media
- ☐ Other: _______________

College 2: ______________________________

Actions I'll take:

- ☐ Attend virtual info session (date: _______________)
- ☐ Request information from the website

- ☐ Connect with admissions rep (name: ________________)
- ☐ Visit campus (if possible) (date: ________________)
- ☐ Follow on social media
- ☐ Other: ________________

College 3: ________________________________

Actions I'll take:

- ☐ Attend virtual info session (date: ________________)
- ☐ Request information from the website
- ☐ Connect with admissions rep (name: ________________)
- ☐ Visit campus (if possible) (date: ________________)
- ☐ Follow on social media
- ☐ Other: ________________

- **Action Checklist: Chapter 2**
- ☐ I understand what data points colleges are using to profile me
- ☐ I've identified important parts of my story that data doesn't capture

- ☐ I've created an intentional engagement plan for my top colleges
- ☐ I know when engagement helps vs. when it's just noise
- ☐ I'm comfortable with the profile I'm building

Completion Date: _______________

Chapter 3 Workbook: Demonstrated Interest in the AI Age

Exercise 3.1: Interest vs. Engagement Audit

Genuine Interest Assessment

For each college on your list, rate your actual interest level (1-5, with 5 being highest):

College Name	Interest Level (1-5)	Why I'm Interested	Engagement So Far

Analysis:

1. Are you spending engagement energy on colleges where your interest is genuinely high?
   ☐ Yes ☐ Mostly ☐ Not really
2. Are there colleges getting too much of your attention relative to your real interests?

---

3. Are there high-interest colleges where you need to increase visible engagement?

____

____

Exercise 3.2: High-Impact Engagement Plan

Quality Over Quantity Strategy

Choose your top 3 colleges and plan 3–5 high-impact actions for each:

College 1: ______________________________

High-Impact Actions:

1. ____

Target date: _______________

2. ____

Target date: _______________

3. ____

Target date: _______________

College 2: ______________________________

High-Impact Actions:

- ____

Target date: _______________

- ____

Target date: _______________

- ____

Target date: _______________

College 3: ______________________________

High-Impact Actions:

1. ______________________________

Target date: _______________

2. ______________________________

Target date: _______________

3. ______________________________

Target date: _______________

Exercise 3.3: When Constraints Are Real

Navigating Barriers to Engagement

Identify your constraints:

I have limited ability to show interest because:

- ☐ Work schedule (hours per week: _______)
- ☐ Family responsibilities (describe: _______________)
- ☐ Limited internet/device access
- ☐ Transportation challenges
- ☐ Financial barriers to travel
- ☐ Other: _______________

Communication Plan:

For colleges I'm serious about, I will explain my constraints by:

- ☐ Including context in the "Additional Information" section of the application
- ☐ Mentioning briefly in an email to the admissions rep
- ☐ Having my counselor address it in their recommendation
- ☐ Explaining during an interview or a conversation

Draft a 2-3 sentence explanation you could use:

____

____

____

____

- **Action Checklist: Chapter 3**
- ☐ I've aligned my engagement with my genuine interest levels
- ☐ I have a high-impact plan for my top 3–5 colleges
- ☐ I've identified any constraints that limit my engagement
- ☐ I have a plan to communicate those constraints when appropriate
- ☐ I'm focusing on depth over volume in my engagement

Completion Date: _______________

Chapter 4 Workbook: Personalized Outreach

Exercise 4.1: Message Analysis

Decoding Personalized Outreach

Save 3 recent personalized college emails and analyze them:

Email 1:

- College: _______________
- Subject line: _______________
- Personal details mentioned (name, location, major, etc.):

- Did this feel genuinely helpful? ☐ Yes ☐ No
- Action it prompted: _______________

Email 2:

- College: _______________
- Subject line: _______________
- Personal details mentioned:

- Did this feel genuinely helpful? ☐ Yes ☐ No
- Action it prompted: _______________

Email 3:

- College: _______________

- Subject line: _______________
- Personal details mentioned:

- Did this feel genuinely helpful? ☐ Yes ☐ No
- Action it prompted: _______________

Reflection:

1. How did these personalized messages affect your perception of each college?

---

2. Did any feel manipulative or pressure-heavy? If so, which ones and why?

Exercise 4.2: Setting Boundaries with Outreach

Managing the Flow

Current State:

I currently receive approximately _______ college emails per day/week.

This amount feels:

- ☐ Manageable and helpful
- ☐ Overwhelming

- ☐ About right, but needs better organization

Boundary Plan:

Actions I'll take to manage outreach:

1. Unsubscribe from colleges where I have zero interest: ☐ Done ☐ In progress
2. Set up filters/folders to auto-sort by priority: ☐ Done ☐ In progress
3. Adjust notification settings:
    - ☐ Turn off push notifications for college emails
    - ☐ Check email at set times only
    - ☐ Other: _______________
4. For high-pressure messages ("Last chance!" "Act now!"), I will:

Exercise 4.3: Turning Outreach Into Conversation

Reply Strategy Template

When a college message genuinely interests you, use this template to turn it into a real conversation:

Template:

Subject: Re: [Original subject line]

Dear [Admissions Rep Name or "Admissions Team"],

Thank you for reaching out about [specific topic from their email]. I'm particularly interested in [specific program/aspect they mentioned] because [brief personal reason].

I have a question: [One specific, genuine question about academics, campus life, support, or opportunities]

[Optional: Brief context about yourself if relevant - e.g., "As a first-generation student..." or "As someone interested in..."]

Thank you for your time.

[Your name]
[Your high school]
[Your city, state]

Practice:

Choose one recent college email and draft a reply using this template:

____

____

____

____

____

____

____

- **Action Checklist: Chapter 4**

- ☐ I've analyzed how colleges are personalizing outreach to me
- ☐ I've set boundaries around the volume and urgency of messages
- ☐ I have a plan for turning helpful outreach into genuine conversations
- ☐ I can distinguish between useful information and sales pressure
- ☐ I feel in control of the communication flow

Completion Date: _______________

Chapter 5 Workbook: AI-Enhanced College Search Tools

Exercise 5.1: Tool Inventory

Which Search Tools Am I Using?

List all college search platforms/tools you're currently using or considering:

Tool Name	What I Use It For	Helpful? (1-5)	Concerns or Limitations

Reflection:

1. Am I relying too heavily on one tool's recommendations?
   ☐ Yes ☐ No ☐ Unsure

2. Have I compared recommendations across multiple platforms?
   ☐ Yes ☐ No ☐ Not yet

- **Exercise 5.2: Building Your List Beyond the Algorithm**

The Complete College List

From AI Tools (Version 1):

Top matches suggested by search tools:

1. ______________________________
2. ______________________________
3. ______________________________
4. ______________________________
5. ______________________________

Wild Cards (Your Own Research):

Colleges you're adding based on personal recommendations, independent research, or curiosity:

1. ________________ (Source: ________________)
2. ________________ (Source: ________________)
3. ________________ (Source: ________________)

Final List Strategy:

My working college list includes:

- ______ Reach schools
- ______ Target/Match schools

- ______ Likely/Safety schools
- ______ Wild card schools

I'm confident this list reflects:

- ☐ My academic interests
- ☐ My financial reality
- ☐ My personal preferences (size, location, culture)
- ☐ A balance of AI suggestions and my own research

- **Exercise 5.3: Comparison Table**

Create Your Own Side-by-Side Analysis

Use AI or manual research to build this comparison for your top 5 colleges:

College	Location	Size	Est. Net Cost	Key Programs	Grad Rate	My Fit Rating (1-10)

Next Steps:

Based on this comparison, I need to:

1. ______________________________
2. ______________________________
3. ______________________________

- **Action Checklist: Chapter 5**

- ☐ I've identified which search tools I'm using and their limitations
- ☐ I've added "wild card" schools beyond algorithm suggestions
- ☐ I've created a balanced list across reach/match/likely categories
- ☐ I've built my own comparison table for top choices
- ☐ I understand that tools advise but don't decide

Completion Date: _______________

Chapter 6 Workbook: Essays, Authenticity, and the AI Question

Exercise 6.1: Pre-Writing Reflection

Finding Your Story Without AI

Before touching any AI tool, answer these questions by hand or by talking them through:

Brainstorming Questions:

1. What's one experience that genuinely changed how you see yourself or the world?

---

2. What do you do that your friends/family would say is "so you"?

3. What's something you've stuck with even when it was hard? Why?

4. When have you surprised yourself?

5. What do you want colleges to understand about your life that might not show up elsewhere in your application?

- **Exercise 6.2: The Voice Test**

Does This Sound Like You?

Write a 100-word paragraph about any topic in your natural voice (no AI):

Now, ask someone who knows you well (parent, teacher, friend) to read it and answer:

1. Does this sound like how [your name] actually talks or writes?

   ☐ Yes, completely

   ☐ Mostly

   ☐ Not really

2. What words or phrases feel most like you?

Keep this as your "voice reference" throughout the essay process.

Exercise 6.3: Setting Your AI Boundaries for Essays

My Essay AI Rules

Before I start drafting, I'm setting these boundaries:

I WILL use AI to:

- ☐ Ask me brainstorming questions

- ☐ Generate an outline structure after I've chosen my topic
- ☐ Point out confusing or repetitive sentences
- ☐ Check grammar and punctuation
- ☐ Other: _______________

I WILL NOT use AI to:

- ☐ Write full paragraphs or essays for me
- ☐ "Translate" my ideas into more sophisticated language
- ☐ Invent details or experiences
- ☐ Generate content I'll submit without heavy revision in my own voice
- ☐ Other: _______________

The "Hand-Write Test":

I commit to being able to recreate my essay by hand, in my own words, if asked. If I can't do that, I've let AI do too much.

Signature: _______________ Date: _______________

Exercise 6.4: Essay Development Process

My Step-by-Step Plan

Week 1: Brainstorming

- ☐ Answer reflection questions (no AI)

- ☐ Talk through ideas with a trusted adult
- ☐ Optional: Use AI to ask additional brainstorming questions
- ☐ Choose my topic

Week 2-3: Drafting

- ☐ Write first draft by hand or typed, without AI assistance
- ☐ Read out loud to myself
- ☐ Share with one trusted reader for feedback
- ☐ Revise based on human feedback

Week 4: Polishing

- ☐ Optional: Use AI to flag unclear sentences or grammar issues
- ☐ Review each AI suggestion—keep only what preserves my voice
- ☐ Read final draft to someone who knows me: "Does this sound like me?"
- ☐ Do the handwriting test: Could I recreate this?

Final Check:

- ☐ I wrote this in my own voice
- ☐ All content reflects real experiences
- ☐ I can explain my topic and main points without notes

- ☐ I saved all draft versions
- ☐ I'm prepared to explain my process if asked honestly

- **Action Checklist: Chapter 6**
- ☐ I've identified my authentic stories without AI
- ☐ I've established clear boundaries for AI use in essays
- ☐ I've written my first draft in my own voice
- ☐ I've had human readers confirm it sounds like me
- ☐ I can pass the "hand-write test" for my essay

Completion Date: _______________

Chapter 7 Workbook: AI in Scholarship Matching and Financial Aid

Exercise 7.1: Scholarship Tool Setup

Platform Checklist

Scholarship platforms I'm using:

1. Platform name: _______________
   - Date profile created: _______________
   - Privacy settings reviewed: ☐ Yes ☐ No
   - Profile completeness: ______%
2. Platform name: _______________

- Date profile created: _______________
- Privacy settings reviewed: ☐ Yes ☐ No
- Profile completeness: ______%

Profile Accuracy Check:

My profiles accurately reflect:

- ☐ GPA and test scores
- ☐ Major interests
- ☐ Activities and work
- ☐ Geographic location
- ☐ Demographic information I'm comfortable sharing
- ☐ Special circumstances or interests

Exercise 7.2: Scholarship Sorting System

The Three-Bucket Method

For the next 20 scholarship matches you receive, sort them:

HIGH PRIORITY (Strong fit, realistic requirements):

Scholarship Name	Amount	Deadline	Requirements Summary	Status

MEDIUM PRIORITY (Interesting but more competitive or time-intensive):

Scholarship Name	Amount	Deadline	Requirements Summary	Status

LOW PRIORITY (Long shots or less aligned):

Scholarship Name	Amount	Deadline	Why Low Priority?

Exercise 7.3: Application Goal Setting

Realistic Scholarship Plan

My Time Budget:

I can realistically spend ______ hours per week on scholarship applications during:

- ☐ School year
- ☐ Summer
- ☐ Specific months: _______________

My Application Goals:

Based on my time and the opportunities, I commit to:

- ______ high-priority applications (target: all of them)
- ______ medium-priority applications (target: 2-3)
- ______ low-priority applications (only if time allows)

Monthly Tracker:

Month	Scholarships Applied	Scholarships Submitted	Notes

Exercise 7.4: Beyond the Algorithm

Local & Community Scholarships

AI tools often miss local opportunities. I will research:

School-Based:

- ☐ Counselor's office scholarship board/list
- ☐ Senior bulletin/newsletter
- ☐ School website
- Local scholarships found: _______________

Community-Based:

- ☐ Parent's employer(s)
- ☐ Community organizations (Rotary, Lions, Kiwanis, etc.)
- ☐ Faith-based organizations
- ☐ Cultural or identity-based organizations
- ☐ Local businesses
- Community scholarships found: _______________

Added Value:

These local scholarships often have:

- ☐ Fewer applicants

- ☐ More personal review
- ☐ Better understanding of my context

- **Action Checklist: Chapter 7**
- ☐ I've set up profiles on 1-2 reputable scholarship platforms
- ☐ I've sorted my matches into priority buckets
- ☐ I've set realistic application goals based on my time
- ☐ I've researched local scholarships beyond AI tools
- ☐ I have a tracking system for deadlines and submissions

Completion Date: _______________

Chapter 9 Workbook: Equity, Bias, and Fairness (For Underrepresented Students)

- **Exercise 9.1: Naming Your Context**

Your Full Story

List the aspects of your life that data and algorithms might miss or misread:

Responsibilities:

- Work (hours/week): _______________

- Family care (describe): _______________
- Translation/support for family: _______________
- Commute time to school: _______________
- Other: _______________

Resources & Access:

- Internet access: ☐ Reliable ☐ Shared ☐ Limited
- Device access: ☐ Personal ☐ Shared ☐ School-only
- Transportation: ☐ Own car ☐ Family car ☐ Public transit ☐ Limited
- Counseling support: ☐ Strong ☐ Some ☐ Minimal

Strengths That Don't Show in Data:

1. ____
2. ____
3. ____

Where to Share This Context:

I will include this information in:

- ☐ "Additional Information" section of applications
- ☐ Essays (where relevant)
- ☐ Conversations with admissions reps
- ☐ Request that the counselor mention in the recommendation

Exercise 9.2: Strategic Engagement for Limited Bandwidth

High-Impact, Low-Volume Plan

Given my constraints, I will focus engagement on ______ colleges (recommended: 3-5).

For each, I'll complete at least 2-3 of these:

College 1: _______________

- ☐ Email admissions rep with brief intro and question
- ☐ Attend 1 virtual event
- ☐ Complete portal tasks promptly
- ☐ Ask specific questions during the visit/event
- ☐ Other: _______________

College 2: _______________

- ☐ Email admissions rep with brief intro and question
- ☐ Attend 1 virtual event
- ☐ Complete portal tasks promptly
- ☐ Ask specific questions during the visit/event
- ☐ Other: _______________

College 3: _______________

- ☐ Email admissions rep with brief intro and question
- ☐ Attend 1 virtual event
- ☐ Complete portal tasks promptly
- ☐ Ask specific questions during visit/event
- ☐ Other: ________________

- **Chapter 11 Workbook: Building a Digital Presence**
- **Exercise 11.1: Digital Footprint Audit**

Google Yourself

Search your name (and common variations) and document what appears:

Page 1 Results:

Result #	Type (Social/News/Other)	Platform	Is This Actually Me?	Keep Public?	Action Needed
1			☐ Yes ☐ No	☐ Yes ☐ No	

2		☐ Yes ☐ No	☐ Yes ☐ No
3		☐ Yes ☐ No	☐ Yes ☐ No
4		☐ Yes ☐ No	☐ Yes ☐ No
5		☐ Yes ☐ No	☐ Yes ☐ No

First Impression:

If a stranger only saw these results, they would think I'm:

Is this the impression I want to give? ☐ Yes ☐ Needs work

Exercise 11.3: Content Alignment

Does Your Online Presence Match Your Application Story?

Your Application Themes:

Main interests/passions you'll highlight in applications:

1. ______________________________

2. ______________________________

3. ______________________________

Your Public Online Content:

What someone would learn about you from your college-facing accounts:

1. ______________________________

2. ______________________________

3. ______________________________

Alignment Check:

Do these match? ☐ Yes, closely ☐ Somewhat ☐ Not really

If not, what can you authentically share online that reinforces your application story?

____

____

____

Exercise 11.4: Clean-Up Action Plan

30-Day Digital Presence Plan

Week 1:

- ☐ Google myself and document results
- ☐ Review privacy settings on all accounts

- ☐ Delete or untag inappropriate photos/posts
- ☐ Unfollow or mute accounts that don't reflect my values

Week 2:

- ☐ Decide which account(s) will be college-facing
- ☐ Update bio/about section on college-facing account
- ☐ Make sure profile photo is appropriate
- ☐ Remove or archive old content that doesn't fit

Week 3:

- ☐ Post 1-2 pieces of authentic content related to my interests
- ☐ Engage thoughtfully with content in my field of interest
- ☐ Google myself again—any changes?

Week 4:

- ☐ Ask a trusted adult to review my main public profile
- ☐ Make final adjustments
- ☐ Set a reminder to audit again in 3 months

Completion Date: _______________

Action Checklist: Chapter 11

- ☐ I've audited my digital footprint through a Google search
- ☐ I've organized accounts into college-facing, personal, and private zones
- ☐ I've cleaned up any content that doesn't represent me well
- ☐ My online presence aligns with my application story
- ☐ I have a plan to maintain a positive digital presence

Completion Date: _______________

Chapter 12 Workbook: Using AI Tools Responsibly

Exercise 12.2: Personal AI Ethics Agreement

My Commitment

I, _______________, commit to using AI responsibly during my college application process.

I WILL:

- ☐ Write all first drafts myself, without AI text
- ☐ Use AI only for brainstorming, organizing, and light editing
- ☐ Keep all content in my own voice
- ☐ Be prepared to explain my AI use if asked honestly

- ☐ Save draft versions to show my process
- ☐ Ask "Could I hand-write this?" before submitting

I WILL NOT:

- ☐ Let AI write essays or substantial parts of applications
- ☐ Submit AI-generated text without thorough revision
- ☐ Use AI to invent experiences or embellish achievements
- ☐ Rely on AI to make decisions that should be mine
- ☐ Share sensitive information with untrusted tools

The Hand-Write Test:

Before submitting anything important, I will ask: "Could I recreate this by hand, in my own words, right now?"

If the answer is no, I've crossed a line.

Signed: _______________ **Date:** _______________

Witnessed by parent/counselor: _______________ **Date:** _______________

- **Exercise 12.3: Application Phase Planning**

Where AI Fits in My Process

Planning & Organizing (AI-friendly):

- ☐ Create application timeline
- ☐ Build deadline calendar
- ☐ Make checklists for each college
- ☐ Organize requirements

Researching & Comparing (AI-friendly):

- ☐ Summarize college website info
- ☐ Create comparison tables
- ☐ Decode confusing terms
- ☐ Generate questions to ask

Brainstorming (AI cautious):

- ☐ Generate reflection questions
- ☐ Explore topic ideas
- ☐ Create essay outlines AFTER I've chosen topics
- ☐ Never: let AI choose topics or generate content

Drafting (AI minimal or none):

- ☐ Write first drafts without AI
- ☐ Write in my natural voice
- ☐ Draw from real experiences
- ☐ Never: paste AI paragraphs

Polishing (AI cautious):

- ☐ Check grammar/punctuation only

- ☐ Flag confusing sentences
- ☐ Suggest clarity improvements that keep my voice
- ☐ Never: rewrite in "sophisticated" style

Exercise 12.4: Practice Scenarios

Is This Okay?

For each scenario, mark whether it's appropriate AI use:

1. I ask AI to generate 10 brainstorming questions about resilience, then I answer them myself.
   ☐ OK ☐ Not OK
2. I paste my essay and ask AI to "rewrite this in a more mature, sophisticated voice."
   ☐ OK ☐ Not OK
3. I write a full draft, then ask AI to check for grammar and repeated words only.
   ☐ OK ☐ Not OK
4. I ask AI to write my activity description because I don't know what to say.
   ☐ OK ☐ Not OK
5. I ask AI to create a simple comparison table of deadlines for my 8 colleges.
   ☐ OK ☐ Not OK
6. I ask AI: "Write a powerful essay about being a first-generation student" and submit the result with

minor edits.
☐ OK ☐ Not OK

Answer Key:

1. OK - Brainstorming prompts, you do the answering
2. Not OK - Rewriting voice
3. OK - Grammar check, you wrote it
4. Not OK - AI is doing your describing
5. OK - Organizing info
6. Not OK - AI wrote the content

Reflection:

Where I might be tempted to cross lines:

How I'll hold myself accountable:

- **Action Checklist: Chapter 12**
- ☐ I've inventoried all AI tools I'm using
- ☐ I've signed a personal AI ethics agreement
- ☐ I understand where AI can help vs. where it should stay out
- ☐ I have a clear plan for keeping my voice central
- ☐ I can explain my AI use honestly if asked

Completion Date: _______________

- **Final Student Reflection**
- **Completion Checklist**
- ☐ Chapter 1: Understanding AI recruitment
- ☐ Chapter 2: Algorithmic profiling
- ☐ Chapter 3: Demonstrated interest
- ☐ Chapter 4: Personalized outreach
- ☐ Chapter 5: College search tools
- ☐ Chapter 6: Essays and authenticity
- ☐ Chapter 7: Scholarships and financial aid
- ☐ Chapter 9: Equity and bias
- ☐ Chapter 11: Digital presence
- ☐ Chapter 12: Responsible AI use
- **Overall Reflection**

What I've Learned:

The three most important insights from this workbook:

1. ______________________________
2. ______________________________
3. ______________________________

What I'm Changing:

Based on this work, I'm going to change:

1. ____________________
2. ____________________
3. ____________________

My Commitment:

I understand that AI is a tool, not a decision-maker or author. I commit to:

- Using it to organize and clarify, not to replace my voice
- Being honest about my process
- Keeping my story authentic
- Advocating for myself while protecting my integrity

Signed: _______________ **Date:** _______________

14.2 Parent Workbook: Guiding Your Student Through AI-Driven Admissions

- **Introduction: How to Use This Workbook**

This workbook helps you support your student without taking over. Each section corresponds to a chapter in the main book and focuses on your role as interpreter, organizer, and advocate—not driver.

What You'll Need:

- This workbook

- Regular conversations with your student
- Access to financial documents for planning
- Willingness to learn alongside your student

- **Chapter 1 Parent Guide: How Colleges Use AI to Find Students**
- **Exercise 1.1: Understanding What Your Student Is Experiencing**

Conversation Starter

Ask your student:

- "How many college emails are you getting each week?"
- "Have any felt especially personalized or creepy?"
- "Which colleges are you actually interested in vs. which are just noise?"

What You Learned:

Your Role:

How can you help your student organize and manage this without taking control of it?

- **Exercise 1.2: Setting Up Systems Together**

Email Organization Plan

Work with your student to:

- ☐ Set up folders/labels in their email
- ☐ Agree on when they'll check college mail
- ☐ Decide what gets auto-filtered vs. manually reviewed
- ☐ Clarify when they should bring something to you

Agreed Schedule:

Your student will check college emails: _______________

You two will discuss together: _______________

- **Exercise 1.3: Privacy and Data Conversations**

Family Agreement on Data Sharing

Together, decide what your student will/won't share:

We're comfortable sharing:

- ☐ Basic academic info (GPA range, courses)
- ☐ Test scores
- ☐ Geographic location (zip code, school)
- ☐ General interests/intended major
- ☐ Demographic information

We're NOT comfortable sharing:

- ☐ Social Security Number (except official FAFSA/CSS)
- ☐ Financial details on third-party sites
- ☐ Social media passwords
- ☐ Other: _______________

Date discussed: _______________
Will revisit: _______________

- **Parent Action Checklist: Chapter 1**
- ☐ I've asked my student about their college outreach experience
- ☐ We've set up an email organization system together
- ☐ We've agreed on data privacy boundaries
- ☐ I'm letting them manage day-to-day, but we have check-in times
- ☐ I understand my role is guide, not manager

Completion Date: _______________

- **Parent Guide: Predictive Yield and Enrollment (Financial Focus)**

- **Exercise 8.1: Understanding Your Family's Financial Reality**

The Budget Conversation

Before offers arrive, establish what your family can realistically afford:

Annual Amount We Can Contribute:

From savings: $____________
From current income: $____________
From student's work/savings: $____________
Total annual contribution: $____________

Comfortable Loan Range:

Maximum total debt we're comfortable with over 4 years: $____________
(Recommended: No more than expected first-year salary in your student's field)

Non-Negotiables:

Our family needs to protect:

- ☐ Retirement savings
- ☐ Emergency fund
- ☐ Support for other children
- ☐ Eldercare obligations
- ☐ Other: ______________

Date discussed with student: ______________

- **Exercise 8.2: Award Letter Comparison**

When Offers Arrive

For each college, fill in:

College	Sticker Price	Grants/Scholarships	Loans Offered	Work-Study	Net Cost	4-Year Total Est.

Questions to Ask:

For each offer:

- Is this aid guaranteed for 4 years? What are renewal requirements?
- What happens if costs increase?
- Are loans federal or private?
- What's the expected monthly payment after graduation?

- **Exercise 8.3: Financial Aid Appeal Preparation**

When to Appeal

We should consider appealing if:

- ☐ Our financial situation has changed since FAFSA (job loss, medical expenses, etc.)
- ☐ An offer from a comparable school is significantly better

- ☐ The gap between aid and our ability to pay is too large
- ☐ Special circumstances weren't captured in forms

Our Story (Brief):

Key financial facts the college should know:

Supporting Documents We Can Provide:

- ☐ Recent pay stubs or tax returns
- ☐ Medical bills
- ☐ Unemployment documentation
- ☐ Other award letters (from comparable schools)
- ☐ Other: _______________

College(s) we'll contact: _______________
Target date: _______________

- **Exercise 8.4: Using AI to Understand Financial Aid**

AI as Financial Translator

Together with your student, use an AI assistant to:

Task 1: Decode Award Letter

Paste the text from an award letter (remove personal identifiers) and ask:
"Explain each line item in simple language and highlight what we need to pay vs. what we're receiving as gifts."

Task 2: Loan Payment Calculator

Ask: "If we borrow $[amount] at [rate]%, what would the monthly payments be over 10 years? How does that compare to typical entry salaries for [field]?"

Task 3: Question Prep

Ask: "Generate a list of questions I should ask the financial aid office about renewal requirements, hidden costs, and special circumstances appeals."

What We Learned:

Important: Always verify AI answers with official college financial aid offices.

- **Parent Action Checklist: Chapter 8**
- ☐ We've had an honest budget conversation as a family
- ☐ We have a clear understanding of our contribution limits
- ☐ We're prepared to compare offers accurately
- ☐ We know when and how to appeal if needed

- ☐ We're using AI to clarify, but confirming with humans

Completion Date: _______________

- **Chapter 10 Parent Guide: Your Role in an AI-Shaped Journey**
- **Exercise 10.1: Self-Assessment**

What Kind of Parent Am I Being?

Rate yourself honestly (1 = Never, 5 = Too Often):

Behavior	Rating (1-5)
I check my students' email for them.	
I write or heavily rewrite their essays.	
I make college list decisions without their input	
I use AI tools on their behalf without telling them	
I contact colleges pretending to be my student	
I help them brainstorm and organize	
I review their work and ask if it sounds like them	

I explain confusing financial information
I advocate when something seems unfair
I step back when they need to lead

Reflection:

Behaviors I need to increase:

Behaviors I need to decrease:

Exercise 10.2: Creating Healthy Boundaries

The Family AI & Admissions Charter

Draft your family's agreement together:

Our Agreements:

1. **Accounts & Logins**
   - Students own their application accounts
   - Parent access: ☐ Emergency only ☐ Shared for review ☐ None needed
   - We keep a secure list of logins at: ________________
2. **Voice & Authorship**
   - Student writes all essays and responses

- Parent/AI role: ☐ Brainstorm ☐ Review ☐ Grammar check only
- Final voice must be the student's

3. **Decision Thresholds**
   Student decides independently: _______________
   We decide together: _______________
   Parent decides: _______________
4. **AI Use**
   - Allowed: _______________
   - Not allowed: _______________
   - We'll discuss before using new tools: ☐ Yes ☐ No

Signed:
Student: _______________ Date: _______________
Parent: _______________ Date: _______________

- **Exercise 10.3: Weekly Check-In Structure**

Regular, Predictable Conversations

To avoid last-minute panic and overstepping:

Our Weekly Check-In:

Day/Time: _______________
Duration: _______________

Standard Agenda:

1. What deadlines are coming up?

2. What's going well?
3. Where are you stuck?
4. What do you need from me this week?
5. What should I *not* do?

Ground Rules:

- ☐ No devices during check-in (or only for reference)
- ☐ Student leads the conversation
- ☐ Parent asks questions, doesn't dictate
- ☐ We end with clear action items for each person

Exercise 10.4: When to Speak Up

Your Advocate Role

You should directly contact colleges or counselors when:

Appropriate Advocacy:

- ☐ Financial information needs clarification or correction
- ☐ Special circumstances need explanation
- ☐ System errors (lost documents, tech problems)
- ☐ Concerns about fairness or bias
- ☐ Your student explicitly asks for your voice

Inappropriate Overstepping:

- ☐ Answering questions meant for your student
- ☐ Negotiating without your student's knowledge
- ☐ Making final decisions for them
- ☐ Impersonating your student

Recent Example:

Last time I spoke directly to a college/counselor:
Purpose: _______________
Was this appropriate advocacy? ☐ Yes ☐ No ☐ Unsure
What I learned: _______________

- **Parent Action Checklist: Chapter 10**
- ☐ I've honestly assessed my level of involvement
- ☐ We have a written family charter on roles and AI use
- ☐ We've established regular, predictable check-ins
- ☐ I understand when advocacy is appropriate vs. overstepping
- ☐ I'm in the passenger seat, not driving

Completion Date: _______________

Chapter 9 Parent Guide: Equity & Bias (For Parents of Underrepresented Students)

Exercise 9.1: Understanding Your Student's Context

Context Documentation

Help your student name realities that data won't show:

Time & Responsibilities:

- Work hours/week: _______________
- Family care responsibilities: _______________
- Commute to school: _______________
- Language translation for family: _______________
- Other: _______________

Resource Access:

- Internet: ☐ Reliable ☐ Shared ☐ Limited
- Devices: ☐ Personal ☐ Shared ☐ School-only
- Transportation: ☐ Car ☐ Public ☐ Limited
- College counseling: ☐ Strong ☐ Some ☐ Minimal

How This Affects the Process:

These factors limit our ability to:

____

____

We want colleges to understand:

____

____

____

- **Exercise 9.2: Equity Questions to Ask**

Practice Questions

Before info sessions or meetings, prepare to ask:

Version 1 (Direct):
"How do you ensure that your use of data and predictive tools in recruitment and admissions doesn't disadvantage students from under-resourced schools or first-generation backgrounds?"

Version 2 (Personal):
"My student has significant work and family responsibilities that limit their ability to visit campus or attend many events. How does your admissions process account for that?"

Version 3 (Specific):
"What support systems do you have in place specifically for first-generation students once they're on campus?"

My Version:

The question I'll ask:

When/Where I'll Ask:

- ☐ Virtual parent session (college: ________________)
- ☐ Email to admissions
- ☐ Campus visit

- ☐ Financial aid meeting

Exercise 9.4: Supporting Without Over-Protecting

Balancing Care and Independence

My Concerns:

What worries me most about my student navigating this process:

Reality Check:

Which concerns are about real barriers vs. my own fears?

Real barriers I can help address:

Fears I need to manage so my student can lead:

My Support Plan:

I will help by:

- ☐ Finding local scholarship opportunities
- ☐ Explaining financial aid letters
- ☐ Asking equity questions when appropriate
- ☐ Helping contextualize constraints in applications

- ☐ Connecting them with mentors/community support

I will step back from:

- ☐ Writing their story for them
- ☐ Deciding where they should apply
- ☐ Fighting every battle instead of teaching them to advocate
- ☐ Over-protecting in ways that limit their growth

- **Parent Action Checklist: Chapter 9**
- ☐ I've helped my student document context data that won't show
- ☐ I've practiced asking equity-focused questions
- ☐ I've researched which colleges show real equity commitment
- ☐ I've balanced my protective instincts with empowering my student
- ☐ I'm advocating alongside them, not for them

Completion Date: _______________

- **Final Parent Reflection**
- **Completion Checklist**
- ☐ Chapter 1: Understanding AI recruitment

- ☐ Chapter 8: Financial planning and yield
- ☐ Chapter 9: Equity and advocacy
- ☐ Chapter 10: Healthy boundaries and roles
- **Overall Reflection**

What I've Learned:

Three key insights from this workbook:

1. ______________________________
2. ______________________________
3. ______________________________

What I'm Changing:

Based on this work, I commit to:

1. ______________________________
2. ______________________________
3. ______________________________

My Role:

I understand my role is:

- ☐ Interpreter - helping decode complex information
- ☐ Organizer - providing structure and systems
- ☐ Advocate - speaking up when appropriate
- **Not:** Driver - making decisions or doing the work

My Promise to My Student:

I will support you by:

I will step back from:

Signed: _______________ **Date:** _______________

Master Checklist (Student and Parent Versions)

- **Student-Only Master Checklist**
- **AI's Impact on College Recruitment**

You can use this as a one-page guide to stay on track.

- **1. How Colleges Use AI & Your Data**
- ☐ I know the main ways colleges get my info (tests, search services, forms, website visits, events).
- ☐ I have a separate, professional email for college and check it on a schedule.
- ☐ My inbox is organized (folders/labels for high-interest, maybe, not interested, scholarships).
- ☐ I understand that my clicks, form fills, and event sign-ups become signals in college systems.

- **2. Algorithmic Profiling & Demonstrated Interest**
- ☐ I understand colleges build a profile of my academics, interests, and engagement.
- ☐ I've picked 3–5 colleges where I want my interest to be clearly visible.
- ☐ For those colleges, I've planned specific actions (events, emails, portal logins, questions).

- ☐ I know my real constraints (work, family, tech, travel) that limit engagement.
- ☐ I have 2–3 sentences ready to explain those constraints in applications or emails.

- **3. Personalized Outreach & Boundaries**
- ☐ I can tell the difference between helpful outreach and pure sales pressure.
- ☐ I've unsubscribed or filtered out messages from colleges I truly don't care about.
- ☐ I have a routine for checking and responding to important college messages.
- ☐ I know how to reply to a good email with real questions to start a conversation.

- **4. College & Scholarship Search Tools**
- ☐ I use at least two college search tools and compare what they recommend.
- ☐ I've added "wild card" schools from my own research, not just from algorithms.
- ☐ My college list has a balance: reach, match, and likely schools.
- ☐ I've created 1–2 scholarship profiles and filled them out accurately.

- ☐ I sort scholarships into high, medium, and low priority and have a realistic application goal.
- ☐ I've looked for local/community scholarships beyond what search tools show me.

- **5. Essays & Authenticity in an AI World**
- ☐ I brainstormed topics without letting AI write content for me.
- ☐ I wrote first drafts of my essays and short answers myself, in my own words.
- ☐ I only use AI for brainstorming questions, organizational help, or light clarity/grammar.
- ☐ I had at least one human reader confirm my essay sounds like me.
- ☐ I can pass the "hand-write test": I could recreate my essay by hand if needed.
- ☐ I've saved multiple drafts to show my writing process if I'm ever asked.

- **6. Equity, Bias, and My Context**
- ☐ I've written down key context about my life (work, caregiving, school resources, tech access).
- ☐ I know where I'll share that context (additional info, essays, counselor letters, emails).

- ☐ I've chosen 3–5 colleges worth my limited time and energy and built an engagement plan for them.
- ☐ I have at least one equity-focused question I'm willing to ask colleges about support and fairness.
- ☐ I understand that being labeled "at risk" is just a prediction, not who I am.

- **7. My Family, My Role**
- ☐ I know which parts of this process are mine to lead (my story, my choices, my voice).
- ☐ I know which parts we share (building the list, visits, understanding money).
- ☐ I know which parts my parent/guardian leads (finances, safety, some logistics).
- ☐ I'm honest with my parents about where I need help and where I need more room.

- **8. My Digital Presence**
- ☐ I've Googled myself and seen what shows up on the first page.
- ☐ I've cleaned up or locked down any public content that doesn't represent me well.

- ☐ I've decided which accounts are "college-facing," which are personal, and which are private.
- ☐ My public profiles generally match the story I tell in my applications.
- ☐ I understand that hateful, cruel, or reckless content can hurt me now and later.

- **9. Using AI Responsibly**
- ☐ I've listed all the AI tools I'm using and what I use each for.
- ☐ I keep AI in an assistant role (planning, organizing, clarifying)—not as the author.
- ☐ I never let AI invent experiences, feelings, or achievements for my application.
- ☐ I make major decisions (where to apply, where to enroll) with people, not tools.
- ☐ I can explain, in 1–2 honest sentences, how I used AI during this process.

- **10. Money, Aid, and My Choices**
- ☐ I understand the basics of sticker price vs. net price vs. loans vs. work-study.

- ☐ I've talked with my family about what we can realistically afford and how we feel about debt.
- ☐ I can compare financial aid offers in plain language (what's free vs. what must be repaid).
- ☐ I know that a big "scholarship" doesn't always mean the cheapest school in the long run.

- **11. Stress, Health, and Perspective**
- ☐ I know my own "stress signals" and what helps me reset.
- ☐ I have at least one adult I can be honest with about feeling overwhelmed.
- ☐ I can name 2–3 things that matter more than the name on my college sweatshirt (values, health, relationships, growth).

---

15 (25) Useful AI Prompts for Students

- **A. College Search, Fit, and Strategy**

1. **Balanced college list**
   "Help me build a balanced college list of 8–12 schools based on my GPA, test scores (if any), preferred majors, locations, campus size, and budget. Label each school as reach, match, or likely."

2. **Discovering overlooked schools**
   "Suggest colleges I might be overlooking that fit this profile: [GPA, interests, region, size preference, campus type, budget]. Avoid only the most famous 'brand-name' schools."

3. **Comparing two options**
   "Create a side-by-side comparison of [College A] and [College B], including majors I care about, campus environment, support services, graduation rates, and estimated four-year cost."

4. **Evaluating 'fit' beyond rankings**
   "Explain the different types of 'fit' for college (academic, social, financial, and personal), and give me a short checklist I can use to rate each school on my list."

5. **Questions for visits or virtual tours**
   "I'm visiting [College], and I'm interested in [major/identity/need]. Generate 15 good questions I

can ask in info sessions or tours about academics, support, and student life."

- **B. Essays, Applications, and Authentic Voice**

6. **Brainstorming essay ideas**
   "Ask me 15 open-ended questions to help me brainstorm college essay topics about growth, challenge, identity, or curiosity. Do not write an essay—ask questions and wait for my answers."
7. **Structuring an existing draft**
   "Here is my rough essay draft. Suggest a clearer structure (opening, middle, ending) and specific places where I should add more detail or cut repetition, but don't rewrite it for me."
8. **Clarity check without rewriting**
   "I'll paste my essay. Point out which sentences might be confusing, repetitive, or off-topic and explain why, without changing my wording. I'll do the revisions myself."
9. **Shortening activity descriptions**
   "Here is a long description of one of my activities: [paste]. Help me shorten this to around [X] characters while keeping the meaning and not adding anything I didn't actually do."
10. **Explaining how I used AI**
    "Help me draft a 2–3 sentence explanation of how I used AI tools in my college application process (for planning, brainstorming, or checking clarity) in a

way that is honest and emphasizes that I wrote my own content."

- **C. Demonstrated Interest, Outreach, and Communication**

11. **Intro email to admissions**
"Write a student-sounding email template I can customize to introduce myself to an admissions representative at [College], mention my interest in [specific program or feature], and ask 1–2 thoughtful questions."
12. **Follow-up after an event**
"Create a short, polite follow-up email I can send after attending a campus visit or virtual session at [College], thanking them and mentioning one thing I learned that increased my interest."
13. **Managing communication overload**
"Help me design a simple weekly routine for handling college emails and texts, including how often to check, which messages to prioritize, and which to unsubscribe from or filter."
14. **Explaining limited engagement**
"Help me write 3–4 sentences I can use in applications or emails to explain why I couldn't visit campus or attend many events (due to work, family responsibilities, or transportation) without sounding like I'm making excuses."

15. **Interview practice**
    "Generate 15 realistic college interview questions and 10 possible follow-up questions so I can practice answering in a way that sounds natural and true to me."

- **D. Digital Presence, Social Media, and Online Footprint**

16. **Digital footprint audit**
    "Give me a step-by-step checklist to review my digital footprint, including searching my name, checking major social platforms, and deciding what to delete, archive, or make private before applying to college."
17. **Designing a college-facing profile**
    "Help me create a basic outline for a college-facing profile (like LinkedIn or a portfolio site) that highlights my interests, activities, and goals in [field], using a tone that still sounds like a high school student."
18. **Aligning online presence with my story**
    "Based on this summary of how I want to present myself in my applications [paste], suggest 5–7 authentic posts or project ideas that would show the same themes on my public accounts or portfolio."

- **E. Scholarships, Financial Aid, and Money Understanding**

19. **Scholarship search strategy**
    "Help me create a scholarship search plan based on my profile ([GPA, interests, location, identity]). Include which types of scholarships to target (local, national, major-specific, identity-based) and a realistic monthly application goal."
20. **Decoding an aid offer**
    "I'll summarize the financial aid offer from [College] (tuition, grants, scholarships, loans, work-study). Explain what each part means in simple terms and estimate my annual net cost and total four-year cost."
21. **Understanding loans**
    "If I borrow $[X] for college, estimate what my monthly loan payments might be on a 10-year plan and compare that to typical starting salaries in [field], so I can see what 'affordable' really means."

- **F. Equity, Stress, and Family Roles**

22. **Describing my context**
    "Help me turn this description of my responsibilities and challenges (work hours, family care, commute, school resources) into a clear, respectful paragraph I can use in an 'Additional Information' section."
23. **Talking about stress honestly**
    "Give me a few sentence starters I can use to talk honestly with my parent/guardian about feeling

stressed by the college process, without it sounding like I'm ungrateful or giving up."

24. **Setting my own AI rules**
    "Help me write a short personal 'AI use agreement' for myself that spells out what I will use AI for (planning, brainstorming, light editing) and what I won't use it for (writing essays, inventing experiences)."
25. **Weekly self-check plan**
    "Create a weekly checklist I can use to review my progress on applications, scholarships, mental health, and AI use, so I can catch problems early and adjust before I get overwhelmed."

---

16 (25) Useful AI Prompts for Parents

- **A. Understanding the Landscape and Your Student's Experience**

1. **Big-picture briefing**
   "Explain in clear, non-technical language how colleges currently use data and AI in recruitment and admissions, and what that means for a typical high school junior or senior."
2. **Conversation starter with my student**
   "Give me 10 open-ended questions I can ask my student about their college process, and AI use that invite honest conversation instead of yes/no answers or arguments."
3. **Understanding demonstrated interest**
   "Explain what 'demonstrated interest' means today, how colleges track it, and what practical, reasonable actions my student can take without burning out."
4. **Identifying my students' constraints**
   "Provide a short worksheet I can use to help my student name real constraints (work, caregiving, transportation, school resources) that affect their ability to show interest, so we can explain this to colleges if needed."
5. **Learning the new vocabulary**
   "Create a simple glossary of key terms (like predictive analytics, CRM, yield model, net price,

demonstrated interest) that I should understand as a parent in this process."

- **B. Healthy Roles, Boundaries, and Communication**

6. **Role self-assessment**
   "Give me a short self-assessment to see whether I'm acting more as a helper/guide or as a 'driver' in my student's college process, and suggest healthier adjustments if I'm doing too much."
7. **Family charter for roles and AI**
   "Help us draft a one-page 'family charter' that defines what my student leads, what we decide together, what I handle (especially financially), and how both of us agree to use—or not use—AI."
8. **Weekly check-in structure**
   "Design a 30-minute weekly college check-in agenda where my student leads, we review deadlines and stress levels, and we end with clear action steps for both of us."
9. **Knowing when to step in**
   "List appropriate situations where I *should* directly contact a college or counselor (for example, financial disputes, system errors, major equity concerns) and situations where I should not."
10. **Talking about AI ethics with my student**
    "Provide 8–10 questions I can use to talk with my student about what we think is ethical AI use in

essays and applications, without accusing or lecturing."

- **C. Supporting Essays and Applications (Without Taking Over)**

11. **Healthy essay support**
    "Explain specific ways I can help with essays (brainstorming, asking questions, checking for clarity) that respect my student's voice and avoid crossing into rewriting or ghost-writing."

12. **Checking voice consistency**
    "Give me a simple method to check whether my student's essay sounds like their normal writing and speech, and how to talk about it if it doesn't, without shaming them."

13. **Talking about AI-written work**
    "Suggest a calm, non-judgmental way to address it if I suspect my student has let AI or someone else write too much of their essay, including questions I can ask and possible next steps."

14. **Helping with short answers and activities**
    "Provide guidance on how I can support my student in describing activities and responsibilities (including work and family care) clearly, especially when they're under-playing what they do."

15. **Managing my own expectations**
    "Help me write a short personal statement for myself about what 'success' in this process really

means for our family, beyond getting into the most selective possible school."

- **D. Digital Presence, Safety, and Reputation**

16. **Joint social media review**
"Create a step-by-step plan for reviewing my students' digital footprint *with them* (not behind their back), including what to look for, how to talk about concerning posts, and how to respect their need for some private space."

17. **Guiding, not policing**
"Give me language I can use to talk about social media and reputation that focuses on long-term impact and safety rather than fear or surveillance."

18. **College-facing vs. personal accounts**
"Explain how I can help my student think about which accounts should be 'college-facing,' which should stay personal, and what the risks are of having everything completely open or completely locked down."

- **E. Finances, Aid, and Yield Models**

19. **Preparing the money talk**
"Help me plan a clear, age-appropriate conversation with my student about what our family can realistically afford for college, including how much we can contribute each year and our comfort level with loans."

20. **Comparing aid offers**
"Give me a template table I can use to compare financial aid offers from different colleges, including cost of attendance, grants, scholarships, loans, work-study, and estimated four-year totals."

21. **Deciding when to appeal**
"List common, legitimate reasons to ask a college to review a financial aid offer, and help me outline a respectful appeal letter structure we could adapt if needed."

22. **Explaining yield and targeting**
"Explain how yield prediction and enrollment models may affect which students get more attention or better offers, and how we can use that knowledge without becoming cynical or manipulative."

- **F. Equity, Bias, and Advocacy**

23. **Advocating for an underrepresented student**
"Provide example questions I can ask admissions or financial aid offices about how they support first-generation, low-income, or underrepresented students and how they try to prevent bias in their processes."

24. **Documenting my student's context**
"Help me turn what I know about my student's responsibilities, school resources, and obstacles into a short, factual statement that a counselor or we can share with colleges for better context."

25. **Supporting without over-protecting**
"Give me practical strategies for balancing advocacy and independence—how to stand up for my student when systems are unfair, while still giving them room to learn, struggle, and own their journey."

---

17 Conclusion

The real goal of this book was never to turn you into an expert on AI or admissions jargon. It was to bring you—student and parent—back to the kitchen table together, with a clearer view of what's really happening behind the screens and a shared sense of control.

For students, you are the center of this whole process. Not the algorithm that sends you a glossy email, not the chatbot answering questions at midnight, not the AI tool that offers to "fix" your essay. You. Your habits, your choices, your voice. If you remember nothing else, remember that AI is just one more tool in a toolbox you already know how to use: you've been learning to Google, to fact-check, to compare, to ask for help your whole life. This is the next step, not a completely different game.

You've seen how AI shows up in recruitment—how your web visits, test registrations, and email opens can turn into a profile that shapes who contacts you and how often. You've learned that "demonstrated interest" is now partly tracked by systems, but still interpreted by people. You've learned that a "personalized" message isn't magic; it's a model doing math on your data. None of that is meant to scare you. It's meant to remind you that you have a say in the signals you send and in the meaning you give them.

You've also seen where AI can actually make your life easier. It can help you build a checklist from a long admissions email, translate financial-aid jargon into plain language, or generate questions for an upcoming info session. It can suggest a timeline, turn scattered notes into a rough outline, or provide interview questions to practice with. When you use it this way—as a planner, a translator, a sparring partner—you are still doing the real work: thinking, choosing, deciding. That's what colleges are hoping to see.

The danger comes when AI starts to feel like a shortcut around that work. It can write smooth paragraphs and polished sentences that sound like someone older, someone different, someone not you. It can make it tempting to paste instead of reflect. But every time it takes over your story, it robs you of the practice you will need in college: explaining yourself clearly, wrestling with your own experiences, and taking responsibility for your words. The more competitive the admissions landscape feels, the more important it becomes to remember that your authentic story—imperfect, specific, human—is still your most powerful asset.

For parents, your role has always been complicated, and AI hasn't made it simpler. You're watching your child walk into a world that didn't exist when you applied to college. There are dashboards and portals, score sends and CRM systems, bots and matching engines, and endless "urgent" emails. It's natural to feel like the only way to be a "good" parent is to grab the wheel and drive. But what your student needs, especially now, is something harder and braver: a steady co-pilot, not a replacement driver.

That means using your strengths—experience, perspective, financial understanding, emotional radar—without smothering their chance to learn. It means reading aid letters side by side, not in secret; asking tough questions about equity and data use, not assuming the school will "just be fair"; helping set boundaries around communication and screen time, not secretly checking their accounts. It means being honest about your own anxieties and history with education, and still making space for your student's path to look different from yours.

Together, you've walked through some of the most sensitive parts of this process: money, fairness, digital footprints, and ethics. You've thought about how algorithms might see you, and how to make sure real people see you more clearly. You've mapped out what you can control—your list, your effort, your deadlines, your voice—and what you can't: admit rates, yield models, policy changes, other people's choices. That distinction is more than a coping strategy; it's a life skill. The families who thrive in an AI-driven admissions world are not the ones who learn every buzzword. They're the ones who get very good at saying, "This part is ours, and this part isn't."

The checklists and workbooks at the back of this book are not meant to be a burden. They're there so you don't have to carry the whole process in your head or in your gut at 2 a.m. They turn vague pressure—"We should be doing more"—into concrete steps: "This week, we'll clean up one social account," "Tonight, we'll compare two offer letters," "Today, I'll write a first draft without any tools." When you cross off those small steps, you're not just moving closer to college; you're building the muscles you'll both rely on long after applications are over.

Because the truth is, AI is not going away. It will be in your classrooms, your workplaces, your finances, your health care. Learning to live with it—thoughtfully, ethically, strategically—is part of growing up in this generation. But there will always be things it cannot do for you: it cannot choose your values; it cannot sit with your disappointments; it cannot replace a conversation between people who care about each other and are trying to do the next right thing. It can draft an email, but it cannot say, "I'm proud of you" and mean it. It can summarize your activities, but it cannot truly know what it costs you to work that job, care for that sibling, or keep going in a hard class.

So as you close this book, don't try to remember every term or every tip. Remember the posture we've been aiming for all along: the student in the driver's seat, the parent in the passenger seat, the AI in the glove compartment—available when you need a map or a flashlight, but never steering the car. Remember that colleges are still full of human beings trying to read human stories as fairly as they can in a complicated system. Remember that your worth is not defined by an "admit" or "deny" button on a screen.

And most of all, remember that this season, as intense as it can feel, is just one season. You will grow through it. You will make mistakes and recover from them. You will learn things about yourself and each other that you couldn't have learned any other way. If you use AI as a **trusted assistant** instead of a crutch, if you stay honest about your process, and if you keep talking to each other even when it's hard, you will come out of this not just with a college destination, but with stronger skills and a stronger relationship.

To every student reading this: you are more than an application, more than an essay, more than a data point in someone's model. To every parent: your steady presence, even with all its imperfections, is one of the greatest advantages your student has in this new landscape.

I wish both you and your parents the very best of luck as you navigate this journey together—and even more than luck, I wish you courage, clarity, and confidence in the choices that are truly yours to make.

www.ingramcontent.com/pod-product-compliance
Lightning Source LLC
LaVergne TN
LVHW010642110826
845149LV00014B/2930

* 9 7 8 1 9 7 2 7 5 2 0 5 0 *